Greg
   It was an honor and privilege to have served as a B-26 pilot in the U.S. Army Air Corps during WW II

1st Lt Ed Ryan

BOMBS AWAY!
MY LIFE AND TRAINING AS A B-26 PILOT

Edward L. Ryon

Bombs Away with sixteen 200 lb. bombs, February, 1945

BOMBS AWAY!
MY LIFE AND TRAINING AS A B-26 PILOT

1st. Lt. Edward L. Ryon
United States Army Air Force
394th Bomb Group
World War II

WALDENHOUSE PUBLISHERS, INC
WALDEN, TENNESSEE

BOMBS AWAY! MY LIFE AND TRAINING AS A B-26 PILOT
Copyright © 2007 Edward L. Ryon. All rights reserved. Cover photograph of Ed Ryon during Primary Training in a Fairchild PT-19 taken by a fellow airman. Photograph of Mr. and Mrs. Ryon courtesy of Olan Mills Studios. Text and cover design, type, and layout by Karen Stone.
Published by Waldenhouse Publishers, Inc.
100 Clegg Street, Signal Mt., Tennessee 37377 USA
888-222-8228 www.waldenhouse.com
Printed in the United States of America
Library of Congress Control Number: 2007926233:
ISBN: 978-0-9793712-6-4

Class 44-D Yearbook cover

Dedication

To Our Wives, Mothers and Sweethearts:

This book, in itself, is a minor insignificant effort. Its meaning, its purpose, if there be such, is entirely personal with us. To you, mothers, fathers, sweethearts and wives, to "our folks" we, the class of 44-D, dedicate this Gremlin. And in so doing it becomes such a great thing, ennobled beyond all measure by the love and devotion linking our lives to yours and yours to ours. How then, shall we put forth in words those thoughts which must herewith be conveyed, except that beyond the heroes, the leaders and the very principles for which we fight, beyond all this, we have chosen to dedicate this book to you.

Taken from The Gremlin, Hicks Field, Fort Worth, TX – Class of 44-D

MY DEDICATION

This book is dedicated to my wife, Margaret, who I have loved and adored most of my life. My love for her grows daily. Without her, this book would have been impossible. She meticulously saved and organized all my war papers and photos.

It is also dedicated to our children, Lindsay Ryon, Jr. and Janice Ryon Lane and their families. Lindsay and his wife, Kaye, have two daughters, Melody and Janna Leigh. Melody and her husband, Paul Gentry, have three boys, triplets, Andrew, John, and Luke. Janice and her husband, Bill Lane, have two children, Ryon and Rebecca.

How could one man be so blessed? Thank God for each of you.

TABLE OF CONTENTS

Foreword	11
Report!	13
New Orders	16
San Antonio	23
The Prayer	25
Primary Training	26
Basic Training	31
Phase Three – Advanced Training	34
Great Days	46
The BIG Day (and life goes on as an Army Air Force pilot)	49
Army Life	53
Off to Europe	61
The Crash	73
Back to Work	77
Paris	81
The Rest of the War	84
Going Home Sweet Home	98
Discharged	104
The Reunion	107
Afterword	111
1st Lt. Ed Ryon's Missions	112
Miscellaneous Photos/Documents	114
Biography	142

FOREWORD

"Bombs away!" As a B-26 crew member, those were some of the best words you could hear during war time. Those words came from our bombardier when he saw the lead plane drop his bombs. Then the crew knew we were closing the bomb bay doors and heading back to the base.

Base – that's been another meaningful concept in my life. I had a wonderful "base" growing up with a great family that afforded me a great "base" in my Christianity. During the war, I had a great "base" with a crew that was with me throughout our tour. I later formed a new "base" with my bride, Margaret. Our love has had a strong "base" and we provided a steady "base" for our new family in Chattanooga.

Without the encouragement of my "base," this book would have never been written. My thanks and love go to you, my family. Our youngest granddaughter, Rebecca, started her Papa off on the computer (what a chore!) by mailing instructions from Knoxville and Chattanooga, Tennessee. A great big thanks goes to Al Rubens, my waist gunner and photographer. He was an encouragement and graciously shared his personal war diary and gave his consent for its use. His anecdotes were often humorous and gave my memory the boost it needed. Another thanks goes out to Susan Neale White, my editing "base," who put this book together for me. She has been an invaluable help, giving of her time and talent. We have enjoyed sharing many afternoon chats with her. Her father, Jack Neale, was one of those "boots on the ground" in the 44th Infantry in World War II and was my good friend and fishing buddy later in life.

And, most importantly, let us never forget the most important "base" of all – the steadfast love and mercy of our God and Lord Jesus Christ.

REPORT!

When I graduated from high school in 1941, the Germans were taking control of all of Europe. The draft was the main topic of conversation everywhere, particularly amongst us young male graduates. We knew our immediate future was planned for us; we would soon be drafted. Bert Arnold, a close friend since grammar school, and I decided we would beat the draft by joining the United States Army Air Force.

It didn't take us long to find the Air Force recruiting office. The sergeant-in-charge was like a long-lost friend, making us feel at home and welcomed. We signed on the dotted line and he scheduled tests – physical, mental, oral, and written – and an appointment with a doctor. Bert passed the tests but I had a fast heart beat. The family doctor, Dr. Blackwell, gave me a little purple pill to take before my recheck. The pill worked and I passed my physical with no problem. We were then told to go home and wait a few days for notification of the time and place to report.

Our first orders were to report at Union Station in Chattanooga, Tennessee. It looked like a bunch of us were going for a ride. There we were met by two men in uniform. One asked everyone with a last name starting with letters A through M to fall in with him. The other took the rest of the alphabet. Doing as we were told, I boarded one train and Bert the other. That had to be the record for the shortest time two friends served together in World War II. We had no idea where we were going or how long it would take us to get there. After a few miles, we figured out we were going south. After a few side tracks and a lot of coal smoke, we finally stopped at Miami Beach.

We stayed in Miami about a month. It didn't take us long to find out what we would be doing. First we were issued uniforms. Size and fit were not a concern – you just had to have a uniform. Next was the assignment of rooms – four to a room in a Miami Beach hotel. Then a short walk (we didn't know how to march yet) to the mess hall.

The routine began. On day two, we were up before daylight and had to fall in downstairs in our new uniforms. After breakfast we went back to our rooms to prepare for inspection. Of course, nothing was right. So, we were told exactly what to do and how to do it. Then it was off to the parade grounds. After more drills, we went back to our rooms to shower and clean up before dinner. After leaving the mess hall, we had time to talk to new friends, write letters, etc.

Day three was the same as day two, and so was day four, five, six, seven, and so on. In a couple of weeks, though, things changed. Officers decided we were ready to pass in review. We were on the parade grounds standing at "parade rest" when the inspecting officers arrived. Several of the cadets (were we cadets then?) passed out from the heat but they sure didn't get much sympathy. Our C.O. (commanding officer) and others finally found their way to the review platform. We marched by and that finished the first review.

We learned things other than marching. We polished shoes, shined our brass, made beds, arranged our foot lockers just right, etc. (all those things a soldier needs to know before going off to combat). We would then wait for the inspecting officer to arrive. The first cadet/soldier to see him would call "Attention!" We would all come to attention by our foot locker at the foot of the bed while the officer inspected uniforms, beds, and foot lockers. If that weren't enough, he also looked for dust and dirt on floors and above doors and windows. He didn't miss a thing. Then came the inevitable explanation of what needed to be corrected.

Just two weeks into the Air Force and I was already finding easier ways to do things. I learned that a little clear finger nail polish on polished brass meant I would never have to polish brass again. My bunk was usually the third to be inspected. One day, though, I was first. The inspecting officer spotted the nail polish on his first step into the room. The polish was a lot harder to remove than to put on. I never tried that again.

The drill sergeant barked at me constantly, saying "Get in step!" After about three or four weeks, he didn't have to yell as much. It was our sign that we had improved a lot. By the last week, we were still marching and drilling most of the time. We were ready for the last time to pass in review. The routine was the same as the first time but I hoped we had improved considerably. Although Miami sounds like a great location for a recruit, we were so busy I don't remember going to the beach once.

NEW ORDERS

We were finished with our month in Miami. Orders were issued to pack and be ready for a move immediately. Nothing hard about that. Just open your duffel bag, throw all your meager belongings in, pull the drawstring, and you're ready to go. Later in the evening, we were on a train heading in the only direction you can go from south Florida – north.

We knew we were out of Florida when, all excited, someone woke us up at about three a.m. It was snowing. Although it was just a dusting on the ground, it was the first snow he had ever seen. We tried to go back to sleep but couldn't. So, we talked until the train stopped in Jackson, Tennessee.

We picked up our belongings, our sole duffel bag, put it on our shoulders and marched to the dorms at Union University. We were assigned rooms and started unpacking. Before we could empty our duffel bags, we fell out for breakfast and marched to the cafeteria. The meal was good – no complaints – but it sure wasn't like home.

Ed on campus at Union University in Jackson, TN – College Detachment Training

With our hunger satisfied, we went back to the dorm and finished unpacking, placing everything in the foot locker just right. We had spare time (sack time, free time, down time, whatever you want to call it) until lunch.

That afternoon was taken up with orientation, the daily and weekly schedules, classes and room numbers, marching and drill, physical training, guard duty, the do's and don'ts, etc. Some of the classes were math (algebra, trigonometry, etc.), physics, geography, English, aerodynamics, engineering, and meteorology. The instructors were mostly civilians while some were Army personnel. They were all very knowledgeable and very fine teachers. They went into depth about their particular subject matter. Just like any school, we had written and oral exams.

One of our outside activities was physical training. Three days a week (Monday, Wednesday, and Friday), we

Ed and Edgar M. Johnson

CTD Buddies with friend

would run cross-country for six miles. Since it felt much longer, two cadets confirmed that distance. Five days a week our training included the side-straddle hop (don't ask me to demonstrate now – I can't!) This training had two purposes – coordination and stamina. But there was more . . . pushups, toe-touches, squats, knee bends, and other calisthenics that I can't remember and sure can't perform today.

Obstacle Course

You never stop marching in the Army. You never stop drills either. We would practice all week for a parade on Sunday. Most everyone in town showed up at the stadium after church and lunch. This was the routine every Sunday. There were no complaints from anyone as everyone in town was extremely appreciative – even the taxi drivers. We would

Inspection

be walking and a taxi would show up, slow down, and the driver would ask, "Where are you fellas going? To the bowling alley? Get in. Just where I'm going. No charge." We never had to pay a fare. They always just happened to be going where we were going.

Mail call was something we looked forward to every day. Mail from home and from Margaret in Cincinnati was regular, something almost every day. It was good to hear the mailman hold up a letter and holler "Ryon!" It was even better when he held up a box of homemade cookies from Cincinnati. I should have thanked all the Fullam family for sharing their sugar and other rations with me.

Guard duty was something

Ed and Edgar

Ed posing with his plane

Ed as a passenger at Union University

new for us and no one took it seriously. If you came in late from walking one of the teachers' daughters home, you just tried not to wake the guard. If you did, all you had to do was apologize and pass on. Bed check was just as easy. There was always someone in your sack by the time the officer looked in. He would never check to see who it was.

Our first plane ride (and it was just a ride) was at Jackson. The teachers and instructors that owned planes would take off with one cadet, circle the field once or twice, and land. This was the only flying we did until primary training. One of the instructors was the artist for the comic strip "Flying Jenny." I have an autographed sketch he drew just for me.

Ed's signed original of "Flying Jenny"

A cadet, Lewis Pendegrass, who retired from the Air Force as a Major and who was from Chattanooga, had to have his appendix removed while we were at Union University. When he was released from the hospital, he was unable to do any physical training and was given leave to rest at home for a few days. He told the doctor he couldn't make it alone and asked if I could go with him. Amazingly, the C.O. gave his okay.

ARMY AIR FORCES COLLEGE TRAINING PROGRAM

44th COLLEGE TRAINING DETACHMENT

Union University
Jackson, Tennessee

Academic record of:

Ryon	Edward	Lindsay
Last name	First name	Middle name

Home Address: Chattanooga, Tennessee *Igod Gap Rd R+ #6*

Date of Arrival _____ Date of Departure _____

SUBJECT	HOURS	GRADE	CREDIT
Physics	68	74	3 Quarter Hours
Mathematics	48	96	2½ " "
Geography	60	76	3 " "
History	20	80	1 " "
English			
Medical Aid	20	90	1½ " "
Civil Air Reg.	28	75	1½ " "

The above quarter hours are not valid if duplication of college work taken prior to entrance into College Training Detachment; or if student had not completed fifteen units of high school work prior to that time.

Gladys L. Stone
Registrar   Mrs. O. D. Stone

Ed's grades at Union Universtiy

When we arrived at Chattanooga, the trains were backed up at the station. We were stopped on the tracks and had to wait. Finally, Lewis suggested we climb out the window and walk to the station. With my help, Lewis had no trouble getting out or walking up the tracks to the station. We had two or three good days at home and then it was back to the books and drills at Union University.

There, they were still marching and singing,

"My girl's a corker. She's a New Yorker. I buy her everything to keep her in style. She has a head of hair just like a grizzly bear.

She has a pair of legs just like two whiskey kegs..."

Another song I remember is, *"Many a night I spent with Minny the Mermaid down at the bottom of the sea..."* This one is worse than my singing, so I'm sure you don't want to hear either one.

SAN ANTONIO

The next move was to San Antonio, Texas for pre-flight school at SAACC (San Antonio Aviation Cadet Center). The nine weeks at SAACC was spent in pre-flight classes, and – guess what? – marching. The classes included aircraft identification, physics, meteorology, Morse code, flight rules and regulations, and aeronautics among others. I'm sure we covered more subject matter than that, but it gets fuzzy after sixty years.

Aircraft and ship identification was one class. There were silhouette slides of planes from every country –

> **Local Briefs**
>
> Edward Lindsay Ryan has been admitted as an aviation cadet for primary flying training at Hicks Field, Fort Worth, Tex.

> **FOUR CHATTANOOGANS AT SAN ANTONIO FIELD**
>
> Four Chattanoogans are now stationed at the Army Air Force Preflight School for pilots at the San Antonio Aviation Cadet Center, San Antonio, Tex.
> They are William R. Davis, 1706 Vance Avenue; Louis A. Pendergrass, 2701 Berkley Drive; Charles T. Ringwald, 1629 Berkley Circle and Edward L. Ryon.

bombers, fighters, twin engine, single engine, dive bombers, and even training planes. These were flashed on the screen for one second, after which we had to write down the identity of the plane and be ready for the next slide. The time of the image was then shortened to one half second, then less and less time. Ship identification was mixed with the aircraft. Ships were much more difficult to identify. Somehow, though, we all managed to finish the course and pass the final exam.

Morse code was a class that gave some cadets a problem. If your mind was a blank slate (no problem for me!) code was not hard. Sending was much easier than receiving. If you sent twenty words a minute, you darn well better be ready to receive twenty. The response would be the speed the correspondent could copy or the speed you sent the code. One could hinder the other. After one session, the instructor asked another cadet and me to see him after class. The other cadet had been copying from my paper. It was as bad to help someone cheat as it was to cheat yourself. He told the instructor that I knew nothing about it. Otherwise, I would have been in as much trouble as he was. I don't remember what happened to him, but it was back to class as usual for me.

Weather is a major factor when filing a flight plan and usually changes from take-off, en route, and at your destination. After getting a weather report (air pressure, humidity, direction and velocity of wind, warm or cold fronts, temperature, clouds, etc.), you figure your heading (the heading can change en route) and ETA (estimated time of arrival). If all your planning is correct, you can get to the destination and back to base safely and on time. When we successfully completed these courses, we were off to the next level of training – primary training.

THE PRAYER

It's hard to remember and get events in the proper sequence, but there's one special memory I would like to tell you about. It was a prayer. I thought about it constantly but three times stand out in my mind – when I prayed, when I was thinking about marriage, and later in combat. I loved and missed my family and thought about and prayed for us all daily. One of my prayer concerns was for my brothers and me. My older brother, J.C., was married and I knew my younger brother, Robert, would be soon after the war ended. If one of us was not to return home, I believed it would be easier on the family if I were the one. I asked God to allow the three of us to come home safely but if one did not, He would choose me. Throughout my training and combat and even now, I have never regretted it. I am just grateful we all returned.

> ### A SOLDIERS PRAYER
>
> STAY WITH ME, GOD. THE NIGHT IS DARK,
> THE NIGHT IS COLD. MY LITTLE SPARK,
> OF COURAGE DIES. THE NIGHT IS LONG.
> BE WITH ME, GOD, AND MAKE ME STRONG.
>
> I LOVE A GAME, I LOVE A FIGHT,
> I HATE THE DARK, I LOVE THE LIGHT,
> I LOVE MY CHILD, I LOVE MY WIFE,
> I AM NO COWARD, BUT I LOVE LIFE.
>
> LIFE, WITH ITS CHANGE OF MOOD AND SHADE,
> I WANT TO LIVE. I'M NOT AFRAID,
> BUT ME AND MINE ARE HARD TO PART--
> OH, UNKNOWN GOD, LIFT UP MY HEART.
>
> I KNOW THAT DEATH IS BUT A DOOR.
> I KNOW WHAT WE ARE FIGHTING FOR:
> PEACE FOR THE KIDS, OUR BROTHERS FREED,
> A KINDER WORLD, A CLEANER BREED.
>
> I'M BUT THE SON MY MOTHER BORE,
> A SIMPLE MAN AND NOTHING MORE.
> BUT, GOD OF STRENGTH AND GENTLENESS,
> BE PLEASED TO MAKE ME NOTHING LESS.
>
> HELP ME, O GOD, WHEN DEATH IS NEAR,
> TO MOCK THE HAGGARD FACE OF FEAR.
> THAT WHEN I FALL--IF FALL I MUST--
> MY SOUL MAY TRIUMPH IN THE DUST.
>
> Author Unknown

PRIMARY TRAINING

We began primary training at Hicks Field, north of Fort Worth, in a Fairchild PT-19. Hicks Field had a long history of training pilots in World War I, then as a helium plant during peace time. It was closed in 1929 but was resurrected as a training base in 1940[1]. The PT-19 was a low-wing aircraft with two open cockpits. This plane could fly at 132 mph and introduced thousands of new pilots to the magic of flight. It was sturdy enough to handle the mistakes of new cadets and capable of aerobatics. So, let's get on to the flying part.

There were four cadets assigned to each instructor. Mr. Acuff was our instructor. My fellow students were Morley K. Russell, Clarence R. McConnaughey, and Harold J. Nanney. They were all a pleasure to fly and work and be with.

Morley K. Russell, Ed, Mr. Acuff, Clarence R. McConnaughey, Harold J. Nanney

McConnaughey, Ryon, Acuff, Russell, Nanney

Soloing was the first challenge. Mr. Acuff, in the rear cockpit, would take off, circle the field, and land. The student, in the front cockpit, would follow Mr. Acuff by lightly holding the controls. Then we would take off, leave the traffic pattern and practice stalls. (A plane stalls when it loses air speed.) We would then return to the air field and try to stall just as we touched the runway. After we got this down pat (usually after six to eight hours), Mr.

---

[1] Freeman, Paul. *Abandoned and Little Known Airfields*: 85/60, Texas – Northwestern Fort Worth Area, http://www.airfields-freeman.com/TX/Airfields_TX_FtWorth_NW.htm

N. Acuff
Instructor

Acuff would stay on the ground and sweat it out while we tried alone. All four of us soloed, taking off and landing several times.

The fun was just about to start. We'd take off, leave the traffic pattern, gain altitude, and then the instructor would demonstrate what the plane was capable of doing. He did straight and level flying, spins, snap rolls, slow rolls, figure eights – more than we knew a plane could do. Then it would be our turn to try. Our attempts did not come out quite like Mr. Acuff's.

Now that we could fly alone, we practiced constantly. In a 90- and a 180-degree turn (or any turn for that matter), the ailerons and vertical stabilizer had to be coordinated. If not, the plane would slide (just like a car taking a curve too fast) and you could feel it and see it on the instrument panel. The controls on all aerobatics had

Primary Training in a Fairchild PT-19

Cadet Ryon

to be coordinated for the maneuver. If you put a plane in a spin heading east, 90 degrees, you pull it out on the same heading. The same went for rolls and most other maneuvers.

Instead of using the compass for aerobatics, we usually lined up with a fence row, power line, or any other fixed object. Figure eights were usually practiced over fence rows or highways or any other landmark that was straight. If there was a cross-wind (side wind), it was difficult to finish over the same fence. After practicing alone

Ed in PT-19

PT-19

for two or three days, Mr. Acuff would give us a check ride to see if we were improving.

Mostly, things went pretty well during the nine weeks we were at Hicks Field. We still had classes. The drills, marching, and reviews never ceased. There were three good meals, time to write home and Cincinnati, and leave the base on weekends. Mail call was still a cherished time of day. I was still getting letters from home and cookies and letters from Margaret in Cincinnati.

There was one accident while we were at Hicks Field. A/C Samuel Schifter overshot the runway and crashed at the end. He died in a demolished plane. I believe this was the only casualty in the training of Class 44-D.

At Hicks Field, we all had the same girlfriend – a "beautiful" donkey named Rosie. Rosie would run and play with you just like a dog would. She would also lift a case of Cokes – twenty-four bottles – one at a time, trying to get a sip from each one. She was always a light-hearted diversion from a busy day.

Ed Ryon in Vultee BT-13

Morley K. Russell in Vultee BT-13

Vultee BT-13s in flight

After nine weeks at Hicks Field, we said goodbye to Rosie and once again packed all our belongings in our duffel bags, pulled the drawstring closed, and prepared to leave for another destination – basic training.

BASIC TRAINING

Basic training in Coffeyville, Kansas was generally the same routine as Hicks Field, but with larger planes, more classes, and more intense training. Our training plane there was the Vultee BT-13, the basic trainer flown by most pilots during World War II. It was the second phase of the three phase training program for pilots. After primary training, a student pilot moved to the more complex Vultee. The BT-13 was a low wing plane with two enclosed cockpits and more instruments. It had a more powerful radial engine and was faster and heavier than the primary trainer. When it started, it really vibrated, so we called it the Vultee vibrator. It required the student pilot to use two way radio communications with the ground and to operate landing flaps and a two-position variable pitch propeller.[2] The instructors were now Air Force officers. It was "Yes, sir", "No, sir", and "No excuse, sir." Those three responses were all you ever needed.

The transition from the PT to the BT was the most difficult for me. My instructor was on leave more than he was on base. He always had a sick mother, a grandmother's death, or some other family emergency. He checked me out solo and I don't remember flying with him again. So, to get familiar with the plane, I would take off, gain safe altitude, and put the plane in a spin. After two or three days of this routine, I felt good about the BT. I was on my own and I really enjoyed it. When it was time for a check ride, any available instructor would ride with me. There were no complaints on any of my check rides.

Instrument flying was coming into our training. The Link Trainer was a major part of this training and new to

Link Trainer

[2.] BT-13 Valiant, from *Wikipedia, the free encyclopedia.* http.//en.wikipedia.org/wiki/BT-13_Valiant

all of us. It was permanently mounted to the floor with a moveable cockpit fully equipped for instrument flying with artificial horizon, turn indicator, compass, air speed, altimeter, and any other instrument a plane might have. Flying the Link Trainer was just like flying a plane on instruments. With the door closed, all you can see is the instrument panel and feel the controls. You take off on instruments, advance the throttle, and level the plane off when you reach air speed. By the time you reach your given altitude, vertigo has set in, and it's extremely hard to overcome that feeling and rely only on your instruments. A 90-degree turn to the right might feel like a climbing left turn or other maneuver. You try to level off for straight and level flight but you could be climbing, descending, have one wing lower than the other or one of a dozen different positions. You must trust the instruments. It was great to get in a Link Trainer but sometimes it was even better to get out.

In addition to our instrument training, the study of meteorology was becoming more intense. Weather (winds, clouds, barometric pressure, etc.) affects all flight plans. Some conditions are very dangerous to a pilot and his plane so we knew we best be attentive and learn.

Nine weeks passed very quickly. It was time to pack the duffel bag again and leave Coffeyville, Kansas. All aboard!

Chapel on base

PHASE THREE – ADVANCED TRAINING

> **Ryon Ends Basic**
>
> A/C Edward Lindsay Ryon, 20, of Chattanooga, Tenn., has completed his basic flight training at the Coffeyville, Kan., army air field and has gone to an advanced field at Pampa, Tex., where he will finish his cadet training and win his wings in the AAF. Cadet Ryon is the son of Mr. and Mrs. James C. Ryon Sr. of RFD 6, Chattanooga.

From Coffeyville, we moved to Pampa, Texas, for our Advanced Training. It was early morning when the train pulled into the station. It had been raining most of the night and half the state of Texas stuck to our shoes as we marched to our barracks. By ten o'clock, the ground was so dry and hard it looked like it had not rained in months. That is the way it was most of the time.

The day started about the same as the first day on any base. We "unpacked" by loosening the string on the duffel bag and dumping everything on the bunk. After placing everything in the foot locker just right, we had a short inspection and orientation. Then things got busy.

Our advance trainer was the Cessna AT-17 "Bobcat." It was used to bridge the gap between single-engine trainers and twin-engine combat aircraft. The "wing loading" was much less than the BT-13. It also had retractable landing gear.[3] We had to get used to two engines, the landing gear, and a slower, lighter plane. As the frame

---

[3] Cessna AT-17, from *Wikipedia, the free encyclopedia.* http://en.wikipedia.org/wiki/Cessna_AT-17

was made of wood and tubular steel, we often called it the "Bamboo Bomber." There was no more aerobatics but other flying was just as enjoyable. We flew on cloudless days in formation. We flew cross country. We flew by instruments and at night. And we learned to never, ever forget your landing gear.

The lead plane was the secret to a good formation. If the lead pilot made all his changes (speed, turns, altitude, etc.) smoothly, it was much easier to stay in a close formation. The wing men forget about their speed, altitude, and turns. They just keep the same distance from the plane they are flying off of. You have to keep your eye on the lead plane constantly. If you are flying off his right wing and he turned right, you turn with him or else fly into him. If he turns left, you turn left or you are out

Ed Ryon in front of Cessna AT-17 "Bobcat"

in the blue all by yourself and it's hard to get back in formation.

There is more than one way to fly cross country. If the weather is clear, you can file a visual flight plan (VFR). You are briefed on the weather, barometric pressure, wind direction and speed, temperature, etc. From this information, you can figure your heading, air speed, ground speed, and estimated time of arrival (ETA). After take-off and en route, you can visually check landmarks to verify that your heading and air speed are correct (or incorrect as the case may be). Once you are over your destination, you make a 180-degree turn back to the base. The wind and ground speed are reversed now. This would have been calculated on the early flight plan.

Cessna AT-17 in the air

An instrument flight plan (IFR) was filed the same as a VFR but the flying was different. All the windows were covered with a green shield. The pilot has red goggles and can see only the instruments. The co-pilot was the lookout but could not help with navigation. You would fly to your destination by your IFR flight plan and the instruments. If your flying and the plan were correct, you would be over your destination at your ETA.

I usually flew cross country with a cadet named Mr. Rust. His name should have been Mr. Right as he was uncannily accurate most of the time. I would try to get him to turn a few degrees or change speed, but he never would take my advice. And "rightly" so. He was always over his target at his exact ETA. I hoped he thought as much of my flying.

Well, I had the inevitable goof. When landing, you enter the airport traffic pattern on the downwind leg, make a 90-degree turn on the base leg, another 90-degree turn into the wind, and you're lined up with the runway on your approach. On the approach you GUMP: that is, you check the (G)as, switch on tank with the most gas; check the (U)ndercarriage, make sure the wheels are down; adjust the (M)ixture, air and gas to the carburetor; and, adjust the (P)ropeller, the pitch of the variable speed props.

This particular day I was flying alone and all was going well. After turning on the approach, I started my check list: G – switched gas to correct tank; U – made visual check of the wheels; M – adjusted the mixture; and P – adjusted the props. On my second check of G-U-M-P, the warning lamp for "U" was off. How could that be? I immediately flipped the switch, visually checked and saw the wheels.

Next, I heard the tower. "Plane on approach, go around. Your wheels are not down." He couldn't be talking to me. I had just checked the wheels. He tried again. "Plane on approach, go around. Your wheels are not down." Still no one was listening. The third time, a loud voice came across, "Plane landing, go around! Your wheels are up!" I glanced out the window and realized he had been talking to me all the time. What I didn't know was that when I flipped the landing gear switch the second time, the gear started retracting. I had seen the wheels just before the gear was going up. I advanced the throttle, went around, and made a safe landing.

After parking the plane, there was a sandwich sign waiting for me. "GUMP" was printed on the front. Guess what was on the back? What else but "GUMP"! I was the chump who had the privilege of wearing the GUMP sign for two days while on flight line. They were kind enough to let me take it off only while flying.

After two days, the officer in charge of the flight line asked – well, ordered – me to his office. The captain asked the reason for this goof-up. I explained the warning lamp and checks I had made on the approach. He had already checked the log and had seen my entry. The crew chief had verified the problem and corrected it. He then asked why I did not come to him with the problem. "Sir, I handled it through proper channels and there was no excuse for trying to land with your wheels up." I was then excused. I saluted, left, and everything was back to normal.

We did most of our night flying in Pampa. We used runway lights and landing lights for takeoff and landing, but the rest of the time it was instrument flying. With the dark nights on the Pampa plains, you couldn't tell if the light you were seeing was a star or on land.

Learning to fly formation at night was scary. All you could see was the exhaust of the lead plane and it was hard to judge your distance. The instructor wanted a tighter formation. I didn't want to turn the controls over to him for fear he'd get too close. We would find the runway lights and land. The remaining part of the night was blissful sack time.

One morning, an instructor met me at the flight line and said, "Mr. Ryon, I'll ride with you today for a little low-level flying." After takeoff, he asked me to drop it down low. We were just over the tree tops and I thought I was doing a fine job of low-level flying. However, the instructor asked for the controls. He demonstrated what low-level flying really was. We were looking up at tree tops instead of down at them. He returned the controls to me and for a while we were just a few feet above ground level. If my low-level flying bothered him, he sure never complained. In my opinion, all instructors should get a medal and hazardous duty pay. They were a brave group.

After weathering a few more sand and dust storms, it was time to start getting ready for graduation. We had to get our uniforms tailored (we all wanted to look pretty). This was the first time we had uniforms that really fit. We received an allowance for our first officer's uniform and then we paid from then on. We notified family and friends and waited for graduation day.

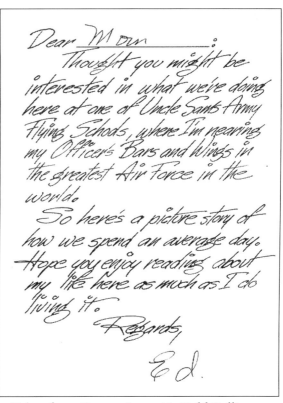

Taken from *Pampa Army Air Field Calling*

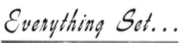

Taken from *Pampa Army Air Field Calling*

Taken from *Pampa Army Air Field Calling*

Taken from *Pampa Army Air Field Calling*

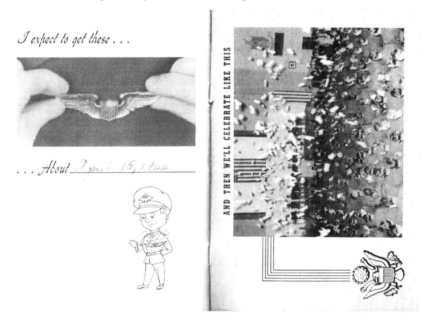

Taken from *Pampa Army Air Field Calling*

Barracks and Life at Pampa Army Air Field, Texas

In front of the barracks, Pampa

?, Morley Russell, Ed   Ed

The Pampa Army Air Field
of
Pampa, Texas
announces the graduation of
Class 44-D
as Pilots Army Air Forces
Thursday morning, April thirteenth
nineteen hundred and forty-four
at ten o'clock

Graduation Invitation

Ethel Ryon (mother), Ed, Clark Ryon (father)

Graduation Day

```
PUBLIC RELATIONS OFFICE                    41844-P13-6C
PAMPA ARMY AIR FIELD                       Times, Chattanooga, Tenn.
PAMPA, TEXAS
```

    PAMPA ARMY AIR FIELD, PAMPA, TEXAS, APRIL 00--When newly commissioned Second Lieutenant Edward L. Ryon, 20, of Chattanooga, received his hard earned silver pilot's wings at graduation exercises at this AAF Training Command's twin engine advanced flying school recently, present to see that they were pinned on correctly were his parents, Mr. and Mrs. James C. Ryon, Sr., R.F.D. # 6, Chattanooga. A 1941 graduate of Tyner High School he was associated with the Combusion Engine Co., Chattanooga, prior to entry into the Army as an Aviation Cadet in August 1943.

-30-

ARMY AIR FORCES TRAINING COMMAND
THE WORLD'S LARGEST EDUCATIONAL SYSTEM

EDWARD F. POGUE

RAYMOND K. BUFFETT

EDWARD L. RYON

JOHN L. PARRIS

LOUIS A. PENDERGRASS

5 CHATTANOOGANS GAIN ARMY WINGS

Commissions in AAF Given at Texas Airfields

Five Chattanoogans completed training recently at Texas and Oklahoma army air fields and were commissioned second lieutenants in the army air forces, it was announced yesterday by AAF headquarters at Randolph Field, Tex.

Those commissioned and air fields at which they completed training are Raymond K. Buffett, 409 Roanoke Avenue, at Altus Field, Okla.; John L. Parris, 5307 Beulah Avenue, at Pampa, Tex.; Louis A. Pendergrass, 2701 Berkley Drive, at Moore Field, Mission, Tex.; Edward F. Pogue, 1002 Woodward Avenue, at Foster Field, Victoria, Tex.; Flight Officer Edward L. Ryon, Route 6, Chattanooga, at Pampa, Tex.

Exercises at 11 Fields

The airmen received their silver wings in brief graduation exercises at 11 flying fields in the central flying training area, with headquarters at Randolph Field. Every state in the Union was represented among the men and Texas led the number of graduates with total of 326 receiving diplomas and commissions. Ohio was second with 298 and Illinois third with 264.

AAF headquarters announced that the recent group of graduates at schools of the central flying command was the largest in the history of the command.

Fighter plane pilots were graduated from the Texas schools Eagle Pass, Aloe, Foster and Moore fields. Bomber pilots came from bomber schools at Waco, Ellington field, at Houston; Brooks Field, San Antonio; army fields Lubbock and Pampa, and from t

GREAT DAYS

Mama and Daddy made the long, tiresome train ride to Pampa to attend the graduation exercise. It was really good to see them and I appreciated them making the trip. All went just as the Army Air Corp had planned. Mama pinned the newly earned wings on me while Daddy watched. Pictures were made and we were ready for the long train ride home to Chattanooga. We stopped in Memphis for a short and enjoyable visit with Granny Ryon, Uncle Dewey and Aunt Mary. After two days there, we boarded the train again and headed for home.

When I got home, things had changed. Well, not really. I was the one that had changed. But everything was perfect as far as I was concerned. I had asked Margaret to come for a visit while I was on leave. After two days at home, I met her train from Cincinnati. From then on, things just got better and better.

Margaret stayed with Sara Elisabeth Ledford at night. But during the day, she was at our house or out just with me. We attended church, went to movies, enjoyed car rides, visited relatives and friends, and the two of us spent hours together talking about nothing and everything. These were some of the best days of my life.

My buddy Bert Arnold was on leave at the same time. We spent some time together before Margaret got to Chattanooga. He was talking about getting married! I tried to tell him that it was the wrong time for marriage but he wouldn't listen. I reminded him that we were going overseas and didn't know when or if we'd be coming home, and how things could change by the end of the war. Furthermore, we were just too young to even be thinking about marriage. But he didn't listen. (Why don't people listen to my words of wisdom?)

Leave was too quickly over and I had orders to report to the Air Force Base at Lake Charles, Louisiana. After giving Margaret a hug and a kiss, I boarded the train. Before the train was out of the city limits though, I was already the most miserable lieutenant in all the United States Army Air Force. The problem wasn't the train ride or my assignment to Lake Charles. The problem was I was in love. I missed Margaret. My letters to her had always ended with "Love, Ed." I now realized what love is.

The only way I knew to get out of this dilemma was to pray and seek God's will. I remember the earlier prayer and knew I might not return home after the war. Next, I wrote a letter to Margaret. (Or was it write the letter and then seek God's will? Hard to tell with a young man in love.) I thought then and know now it was indeed God's will. This all occurred on the first part of the train ride to Lake Charles.

Now, as for the letter, it was hard to write. I wasn't nervous; it was just that the train ride was bumpy. (Well, maybe I was a little nervous too.) Of course, the main topic was "I love you. Will you marry me?" A few more sentences and then I signed it, "LOVE, Ed." After waiting four or five long days, I nervously opened the letter from Margaret. Her answer was "yes" with the condition that we would live in Chattanooga. (She never did like Cincinnati.) Well, her true answer was "yes" if I would get her dad's permission. So, I wrote one more letter to her dad but I was feeling good about everything now. Margaret's dad didn't write. He just gave her the OK.

As it turned out, I didn't even follow my own advice. I got married one month after my buddy Bert.

Ed with his father, James Clark Ryon

Ed with his aunt, Mary Ryon Harrison

Ed and Granny Ryon

Ed and Margaret Fullam

THE BIG DAY
(and life goes on as an U.S. Army Air Corp pilot)

I was getting all ready for the wedding in two or three days, meeting with the preacher and arranging the day and time. WRONG! I should have consulted with my bride-to-be. There was an engagement ring and other details I didn't know about to be taken care of. But, whatever it was, the big day was delayed for about three weeks. The date was set for June 17, 1944.

TROTH ANNOUNCED FOR MISS FULLAM

Cincinnati Girl Will Marry Edward Ryon of This City

Mr. and Mrs. Frank L. Fullam of Cincinnati, Ohio, formerly of Chattanooga, announce the engagement of their daughter, Miss Margaret Elizabeth Fullam, to Flight Officer Edward Ryon. The wedding will take place the latter part of this month in Shreveport, La.

The bride-elect is the sister of Miss Barbara Ann Fullam, Carolyn Fullam, Frank Fullam Jr. and S/Sgt. Raymond Fullam, now serving with the army air forces in India. She is a graduate of the Withrow High School in Cincinnati and attended the University of Cincinnati. Mr. and Mrs. Leland Fullam Sr. of this city are the birde-elect's grandparents.

Flight Officer Ryon is the son of Mr. and Mrs. J. C. Ryon of East Brainerd. He is the brother of Misses Genevieve and Margaret Ryon and Pvt. J. C. Ryon Jr. a Pvt. Robert Ryon, who are stationed in England. He graduat from Tyner High School and ceived his wings and commiss from the Tampa Air Field, Tam Fla. He is now stationed Barksdale Field, Shreveport.

MISS MARGARET ELIZABETH FULLAM'S engagement to Flight Officer Edward Ryon of East Brainerd is announced today.

The wedding was to be at the First Baptist Church in Lake Charles with Rev. Stagg officiating. The preacher had several questions he wanted answered before he agreed to perform the marriage. I explained to him that we had known each other all our lives, our parents knew and approved our plans, and we were both Baptists and wanted to get married in a Baptist church. But, I said, we would go elsewhere if we had to. So, he finally agreed.

While waiting for June 17 to roll around, we were flying one fine plane. The B-26 Martin Marauder was truly a lady – one of the best. She had two Pratt & Whitney R-2800 radial engines. The wing span was 65 feet, which was later increased to 71 feet. She had a loaded weight of approximately 37,000 pounds. The wing loading was more than other bombers. Takeoff speed was at 145 mph. The maximum speed was about 300 mph while cruise speed was about 220 mph. When landing, the approach was 130 mph and touch down was about 90 mph. Combat range was 1,150 miles and ferry range was 2,850 miles.[4.]

The B-26 was well equipped for combat. She could carry a 4,000 pound total bomb load of different variations – two 2,000, four 1,000, eight 500, etc. She had eight 50-caliber machine guns for fighter protection – two in the tail, two in the waist, two in the dorsal turret, and two in the nose. There were four fixed guns on the sides of the fuselage for strafing. These were operated by the pilot. She had several nicknames, most of them bad. She was known as "the Widowmaker," "the Flying Coffin," and "the Prostitute" (because, with her short wings, she had no visible means of support). Due to the rotund fuselage, the B-26 engines were placed far outboard. Loss of power on one side would result in a violent snap roll, flipping the aircraft on it back. This led to a high number of accidents during takeoff. The personnel at MacDill Air Field in Tampa, Florida (where pilots trained) would say "One a day in Tampa Bay."[4] But the beautiful B-26 lived through it all and was a fine plane.

[4.] B-26 Marauder, from Wikipedia, the free encyclopedia. http://en.wikipedia.org/wiki/B-26Maurauder

Once you started your pre-flight and were in the plane, you fell in love with it, just like a kid with a new toy. At just twenty-one years old, we were kids with a BIG new toy. Once in the cockpit, you began the routine – checking the fuel, controls, seat belts, and so on. Once that was done, you were ready to start the engines. The pilot would look left for ground personnel and after seeing none in danger, he yells "Clear left!" and starts the left R-2800. It starts its slow turn, fires, and starts. You now have 2000 horsepower under control. The process is repeated for the right engine. With brakes on, you check your flaps and vertical and horizontal stabilizers. Once you are sure the yoke is free and everything is operating properly, the brakes are released and the plane starts moving. The throttles are advanced ever so slightly to taxi to the end of the runway. While still on the taxi strip, you make your final checks before takeoff. Lock the brakes and check the engines at full power. Check the manifold pressure, the cowl flaps, the RPMs, wing flaps, trim tabs – there is a whole checklist.

Once on the runway, you advance the throttles, release the brakes, and the winged beauty starts to move forward with increasing speed. As the throttles are moved to full power, you have 4,000 horsepower under your control. In a few seconds, you are moving at 145 mph. With a slight pull on the controls, you are airborne, as smooth as silk.

As this is a short flight, it's time to land. The traffic pattern is entered on the downwind leg. Then you turn left on the base leg. The next left turn will be into the wind on the approach. You're now lined up with the runway. Decreasing power and adjusting the wing flaps causes the plane's airspeed to drop to 150 mph, then on down to about 90 mph for touchdown. After taxiing and parking the lady, you get out and wonder how you ever accomplished this.

First Baptist Church, Lake Charles, LA

Finally, the big day arrived. The wedding was the afternoon of June 17, 1944. It was attended by my sisters, Jenieve and Margaret from Chattanooga, and several officers from the air base. Lt. Albert Kiser was my

Margaret and Ed between Ed's sister, Jenieve, on left, and Margaret

best man. The ceremony was short but thorough and the bride made it the most beautiful ceremony ever. There were no plans for after the wedding except for pictures. I hadn't even made plans for dinner. So we had a seafood dinner, Louisiana style. It was a very enjoyable meal to end a most wonderful day. Now we could settle down to Army life.

Wedding Day Groom's Party. Best Man Lt. Albert Kiser is center back

ARMY LIFE

I had rented one room and bath in a private home close to the base. It was as comfortable as could be with no air conditioning. (Nothing was air conditioned back then.) It was "air cooled," though, with a six-inch fan in the window. The fan made more noise than a B-26. We discovered a drop of Brilatine hair oil would stop most of the noise. This only lasted two or three hours before another drop of oil was required. A fan blowing 100 degree outside air into 100 degree inside seemed to help a little, but only a little.

We needed (or wanted) transportation. So, with our best friends, Alton and Edna Parsons, we paid $600 for a 1936 Ford convertible. We were now big shots with a convertible. We could drive to the Officers' Club for dinner, around the block to play tennis, or any "important" place we needed to go.

Margaret with the 1936 Ford convertible

We had time to make short trips. We had never seen the Gulf of Mexico, so the four of us were off on our way. We didn't need a map because we knew it was south. We were bound to run into it sooner or later. We were on the highway and the compass indicated we were going south. After a few miles, we were on a two-lane paved road. Then it became an unpaved road; then one lane. If we found a place to turn around, we were going to abort this mission and return to the base.

The turnaround and the Gulf came into view about the same time. To get to the Gulf would be a mile walk through high grass, weeds, and sand. Well, we had now seen the Gulf and decided to use the turnaround and made it to the Officers' Club in time for dinner. Margaret learned not to wear shorts in the Louisiana sun in a convertible with the top down.

I don't know who initiated the plans for the next trip but we all agreed on it. Alton's sister lived in Etowah,

The Parsons & The Ryons

Tennessee. Margaret and I would stop over in Chattanooga. Alton and Edna would go on to Etowah. In two days, we would start our return trip.

We had three strikes against us. Gas was rationed and we didn't have enough gas stamps to get us near halfway. We had five recapped tires. And the car really had a "rag" top. We decided to make the trip anyway. Just in case, we made arrangements with friends to call home or Alton's sister if our name came up to "ship out" or any other assignment. With that "careful" planning, we were on our way.

When we stopped for gas, most stations would not take our gas stamps. In fact, they would ask if we needed more. So, we were getting stamps and using very few. The weather was clear and the tires were holding up okay. We had only one little problem on the way up. We took a wrong turn in Baton Rouge and lost about half an hour. Regardless, we had a good trip the rest of the way to Tennessee. Alton and Edna dropped us off in Chattanooga and were on their way to Etowah.

As planned, after two days we were on our way back to Lake Charles. Alton had had tire trouble between Chattanooga and Etowah so we were down to four recaps. Also, he wasn't feeling very well. Alton and Edna moved to the back seat, and Margaret and I took the front. In a very short while, he was sick and laid down for the entire trip back to Lake Charles.

We were driving back at night and things were going well until it started raining. The rain increased until it was a downpour. The car top leaked so much you couldn't tell if it was up or down. We were so wet that I pulled off my

Edna & Alton Parsons

Alton Parsons & Margaret

Ed with Alton Parsons

Edna Parsons and Margaret

shirt and Margaret used it to keep my face and the windshield as dry as possible. It was a losing battle, though. But we had to keep going.

There was more trouble to come. The headlights were getting dimmer all the time. The generator had given up. In the end you couldn't tell the lights were on. We had to get back to the base so we slowed down and kept moving. The lights from Lake Charles never looked so good! We were AWOL for days and no one missed us. The next day we slid back into our regular routine – eat, check the roster, then tennis, movies, or some flying three or four times a week. (The car's generator did get repaired.)

On one training flight, we (the five crew members I would be flying with permanently) landed at Meridian, Mississippi, and had to spend the night. I don't remember why. It could have been the weather, engine trouble, or some other problem. The group going to dinner that night at Lake Charles would be one short. I wasn't concerned, though, because Lt. Rollia was a perfect gentleman and escort. He would see that Margaret got to the Officers' Club and back home safely.

A few nights later, Rollia didn't make it to dinner with us. Driving home, we saw a plane crash and drove by to get a better look. That was a mistake. It was the plane Lt. Rollia was flying. There were no survivors. This was hard on all of us, especially Margaret and Edna. We managed to put it behind us after a few days. Rollia was the only close friend that lost his life while still in training.

One morning the duty roster listed "LT Ryon, Edward L., Airdrome Officer" for the day. I didn't know we had airdrome officers, much less their duties. My first stop was the tower at the airport. I admitted to the sergeant that I had no idea what my duties were. It took him two minutes to explain them to me: (1) See the jeep on the ground? The keys are in it. If you want to, ride to the end of the runway and look for trash or uneven pavement. It is alright. I can see from here; (2) Leave a phone number where I can get in touch with you. If some high-ranking officer lands, you'll need to meet his plane and give whatever assistance he needs. I left my phone number, inspected the runway, and drove the jeep home.

The day was spent near the phone. Mid-afternoon, the tower called and notified me that I needed to meet a plane in half an hour. I was waiting by the plane when the pilot cut the engines. A naval officer, also the pilot, returned my salute and asked to go to headquarters. I was to pick him up in one hour. I was five minutes early. He was on time – not late, not early - exactly on time. At the plane, he thanked me, started the engines, and taxied for takeoff. This was the only duty I had other than flying while in the U.S.

In Lake Charles, we were on the tennis courts quite a bit. I liked to be with Margaret even if she did win consistently. One hot day (all days were hot in Lake Charles), we started walking home from the courts. Just as we stepped off the sidewalk onto the street, Margaret fainted. Kerplop! She hit the street. With no warning that anything like this was about to happen, I didn't know what to do. There was only one person in sight and she was there in a second. We got the patient on a bench nearby and in a few minutes we were ready to start walking again. I don't remember seeing the lady after she helped us. This was the one and only time I ever thought of running off.

We were at Lake Charles for about six weeks when orders came for us to report to Hunter Air Force Base in Savannah, Georgia. We were asked/ordered not to bring

Rickmyer, Ed Ryon, Lew Kraft, Manny Ranier, Dick Hoyal, Al Rubens

our wives because we were only going to be there for a day or two. At Hunter, things changed and we were to be there much longer. With two phone calls, one to Tennessee and one to Kentucky, Margaret and Edna were on the train to Savannah.

Our few weeks in Savannah were a very delightful time. We flew twice, maybe, and the rest of the time was free to do as we pleased. The time was spent walking, talking, and sight-seeing. One evening, Margaret and I ran into the other five crew members on the street. We stopped and started chatting. Everyone walking by would smile as they passed. Finally, Manny, the turret gunner, walked around to see why all the big smiles. Margaret had on a new suit and had failed to remove the tags. I clipped the tags for her, and we received no more smiles.

One day on the waterfront, a ship was being launched. Alton, Edna, Margaret and I stopped to see something we had never seen before and would likely never see again. The naval officers asked us to join them on the viewing platform. The ceremony was carried out to perfection. The four of us were able to take part in this thanks to the Navy. We expressed our appreciation to the Navy, left the platform, and went back to watching the side shows taking place between the waterfront and the street. After about a month of this "difficult" assignment, orders came for one more move.

OFF TO EUROPE

On October 6, 1944, we were asked to report to the flight line and get prepared for takeoff. We were then assigned a plane and given sealed orders that were to be opened after takeoff. The orders gave us our destination and route. We were going to Stone, England.

Before leaving Georgia, I wrote Mama and made arrangements to have flowers sent to Margaret on the seventeenth (remember, we were married on the seventeenth) of each month until I returned. She never missed a month.

There were no nonstop flights for a B-26 from the U.S. to England. We flew the southern route to South America, Ascension Island, Africa, and on to Stone, England. The first leg from Hunter Field was an enjoyable, smooth ride. We landed in the city of Natal, Brazil. This was the first time any of us had been outside the United States. The layover in Natal was to be short. We had time to eat and sleep and prepare to leave the next morning.

Ascension Island is one little speck of land in the middle of the Atlantic between South America and Africa. Our crew – the pilot, co-pilot, and navigator – made our flight plans and hoped they were correct. We took off and set our heading for the island. Everything was going fine until the right engine started giving us trouble. The oil pressure was dropping. I couldn't synchronize the props and it was losing power. So we made a 180-degree turn back to Natal. We radioed the tower in Natal, reported our trouble, and gave them our ETA.

When the field came into sight, they were ready. The runway was cleared, rescue personnel lined the runway, and the tower gave us the green light to land. Rick made a perfect landing; he was one of the best. We all got out of the plane, glad to be on solid ground. The ground crew moved the plane to the repair shop. The next morning we were ready to try again.

We used the down time to sightsee and shop. I found some beautiful silk in Natal, and I sent a couple of bolts to Margaret. I also bought her some silk hose and a bottle of Chanel No.5 (You couldn't buy hose or perfume in the U.S.) and a few other keepsakes. I'm sure Margaret wore the hose out. The perfume was broken on her train ride back to Cincinnati. That was one sweet-smelling train car! She still has the other things from Natal.

An aside here. It had been months since I had received a letter from Margaret. There was no need to write as we were always together. From the day I flew out of the

> France
> Jan 17, 1945
>
> Dear Mom,
>
> I got my pen fixed to day & it's sure fine. I like it better than any present I've got so far. I had a time explaining to the guy in town what was wrong with it and what I wanted done but I finally made it.
>
> I have my laundry done by a lady up the street. She's real nice & we have a time explaining what we want. I wanted her to make me a scarf to day and I like to have never got her to understand me. I usually make out okay after a while.
>
> She's got a girl about 8 or 9 years old and she's as cute as she can be. We usually take her some candy, gum, or some thing when we have it to spare. That's my girl until I get back to Punkin.
>
> In a day or two I'm going to send home some money and I want you to do some thing for me. On the 11th of every month (or so they'll get there on the 11th) I want you, or Jen, or Marg. to send Punkin some

Letter to Mom asking her to send flowers to "Punkin" once a month.

States until the day I returned, Margaret wrote every day, the letters often accompanied by cookies. I didn't get mail every day. Some days there was one letter, some days no mail, and some days three or four letters at once. But it all averaged out to at least one letter a day.

> flowers. I don't care what kind, but we can't get anything here and I want to send her something. Put on the card "Love and Kisses – Ed."
>
> That's about all I can think to write now so I'll close & try to write more to morrow.
>
> Goodnight & Love
> Ed.
>
> PS. I guess I should tell you I'm okay and every thing fine
> PS. JR. I'm okay & everything is fine.
> PS. III Richtmyer is 1st Lt. He made his first the 8th of Jan.

Money for flowers for a year

After breakfast the next morning, we were off to try to find that speck in the middle of the ocean again. As it turned out, it really wasn't hard to find. We flew our heading until we heard their radio. We tuned our radio compass to the signal, and it pointed straight to the island. The island always has a cloud cover, so we lowered our altitude, came in under the cloud cover, and landed. There was nothing to do there but eat, watch a movie, and wait.

Our next leg was to Dakar, a small peninsula on the western coast at the widest part of Africa. Dakar was a small, hot, dirty place. I watched one snake charmer and had seen enough. We were all more than ready to start our last leg to England.

We flew north and saw England and found the town of Stone. The main thing I remember about Stone, England was the airplanes. I have never seen so many planes in one place in all my life. After landing, we taxied and followed a jeep to a parking spot. I don't think we ever saw this plane again. The stay in England was short.

Soon we were on a C-47 heading southeast. (Was the pilot sure of his heading? I heard there was a war in that direction.) We landed at an air field near Paris, France. We had dinner and were assigned a place for the night – a cot in a tent. All was going well until we started hearing rifle fire. There were still a few snipers close by. I was right; there was a war going on. I don't believe the snipers had targets. They were just trying to unnerve us. One round put a hole in the tent. No one was injured in this small incident that I know of. In spite of it all, I got a good night's sleep.

Cambrai, France, was our next stop. It was from this air field that we flew all of our missions. Our living quarters were in a convent. It was nice and comfortable with room to move about and was just a short walk to town.

Meals were good except for breakfast at times. If breakfast was "ski wax" (oleo) and waffles and "s--- on a shingle" (toast), we passed it up.

Rick and I were in a room with four other lieutenants who had been there a while and knew all the ropes. They had made friends with a family at the edge of town, and we traded soap (mostly) for eggs. With this addition, all our meals were fine.

Our first flight from Cambrai was very short. We needed to see the difference in the landscape of France and what our new home looked like from the air. I kept my eye on the air field constantly. I was anxious to get back on the runway.

Too soon we were scheduled for a mission. Usually the routine was up early, breakfast, briefing, and then to the flight line and the assigned plane. We didn't fly the same plane every time. All briefings were about the same; only the time, route, and target changed. The target could be one of many things – a bridge, ammo dump, train, factory, convoy, or anything that would help the war effort. Most of our targets were bridges, busy crossroads, or marshalling yards. The route to the target was never a straight line. Intelligence knew where all the enemy fighter bases were, the location of all stationary anti-aircraft guns, and usually the movement of mobile anti-aircraft guns. A zigzag route was planned to miss all of these.

The first mission was the one you always remember. We climbed into the plane, each crew member checking his equipment. The engineer was the gunner for the turret gun on top of the plane. The waist gunner also doubled as the photographer. The tail gunner, also the radio man,

Ed in Cambrai, France   Ed and Rick

was in a very small area with little wiggle room. The bombardier was also the navigator; his station was in the nose of the plane. The pilot was in the left seat of the cockpit and I, as co-pilot, was in the right seat. We were now ready to start our engines. But first, I bowed my head and prayed as I did before every mission I flew.

When it was time, we started and checked our engines and taxied with other planes to the runway for take-off. On the runway, one plane would take off from the left side. Seconds later, the next would leave from the right side. When airborne, we started getting into formation – six in a flight. Then the flight would join the squadron.

We didn't know what to expect on our first mission. The lead plane, the only plane with a bomb sight, found the target, made the bomb run, and dropped his bombs. The other five planes dropped theirs when they saw the lead plane's release. We then turned toward the base and headed home. After debriefing, the mission was complete. The first mission was a "milk run." We saw no enemy fighter, no flak, no planes lost, and we destroyed our target. The second mission was about the same, no problem whatsoever. This wasn't as bad as I thought it might be! Just think, sixty-five of these and I'll be on my way home.

Mission three was different. One plane received a direct hit by flak. It looked like a crumbled cracker. Parts were falling everywhere. I think that was the only loss on that mission. In a few days I saw this happen again. I stopped thinking about sixty-five missions and started thinking about them one at a time. (When I was assigned to fly, they would find me hiding under my bed, in the latrine, and once in the kitchen with an apron on. But they always found me. Just kidding! The truth is, when I was scheduled to fly, I would do what we were trained to do and what everyone else did – complete the mission and expect the same the next day.)

Al Rubens, the waist gunner, kept a diary of each mission, giving the target, the weather, flak and enemy fighters, loss of aircraft, etc. Each mission started the same. The flight plan was laid out at the briefing. We were given the target and where to expect flak and fighters. Staying on flight plan was stressed. Flak was expected on most missions; fighters not as often.

I wish I could remember the target or date of this mission. It would make it easier to write about. The briefing and the flight to the target are what I distinctly recall.

The target was north-east of Cambrai. However, since there were stationary AA (anti-aircraft) guns in the direct flight path, we were to first fly east and then turn north. On the first leg (east), we would be flying between and out of range of the guns. Then on the turn north, we would be behind other stationary AA guns. During the briefing, we were also told about some mobile guns to the south of the leg, but the briefers did not think those guns would cause any trouble for us.

Take-off and getting into formation was, as usual, no problem. We headed east into clear blue skies. Soon, though, we were getting some light, accurate flak. We knew that in a short time we would be behind the AA guns stationed in a line north and south of us. So we forged ahead. We turned north at the correct time and distance to stay out of range of the AA guns. Yet, the flak was now heavy and accurate and stayed with us to the target. We dropped our bombs and were to return to the base following the same course. The flak stayed with us on our return trip also.

Surprisingly and thankfully, we did not lose any planes. Several had considerable damage, though, mostly small holes in the fuselage. It still amazes me how so much flak could cause so little damage. We were fortunate this time. How could it be that we encountered so much flak? Was it navigation, briefing, intelligence, or just lucky Germans that happened to be in the right place at the right time? As a soldier and a pilot on the front, you learned not to worry about it. Tomorrow would be another day with another story to tell.

The best defense from fighters was a tight formation. One B-26 had eight guns that could be fired at a fighter.

That meant forty-eight guns in a flight and many more in a squadron. What fighter pilot would want to fly into that?

The bombardier in the lead plane had control of the planes on the bomb run. The bomb run started on the approach to the target. The plane had to be in straight, level flight which made us an easier target for enemy anti-aircraft guns. The bombardier located the target in his bomb sight and made slight changes in the planes' heading as needed. Taking altitude into consideration, he calculated when to drop the bombs. The five other planes in the flight dropped their bombs when the lead plane dropped his. Pattern bombing would usually hit the target. It was always good to hear "Bombs away!" That was our cue to make a 180-degree turn and head home.

There was another mission I remember very well. When a new crew came into our squadron, a pilot that had flown several missions was assigned to their crew for the first mission. This was the only time I flew with a different crew. I met the pilot and bombardier at the briefing and the rest of the crew at the plane. After boarding the plane and buckling my seat harness, there was time for a short prayer, as usual, before starting the engines.

After take-off, we took our place below the formation as one of the window ships. Our payload for this flight was "slightly" different. We were not loaded with bombs. Rather, we were loaded with bundles of tin foil cut to the length of the enemy's radar wavelength. The waist gunners on the three window ships would toss the bundles out while the pilot made S-turns under the formation. The radar-controlled guns on the ground couldn't tell if they were shooting at aircraft or tin foil.

All went well until the bombs were dropped and we headed home. Over friendly territory, we lost one engine. The propeller on the dead engine was feathered (Feathering means to turn the blade approximately parallel with the line of flight, thus equalizing the pressure on the face and back of the blade and stopping the propeller. Feathering is necessary if for some reason the propeller is not being driven by the engine and is windmilling, a situation that can damage the engine and increase drag on the aircraft).

We lost a little altitude but we would be able to return to the base on one engine. In a very few minutes, the other engine stopped. Now, the glide path of a B-26 is about the same as that of a rock. So, over the intercom, I asked the crew to get prepared to bail out. We were over mountains, but the pilot had spotted a small field under the left wing, and he asked us all to get in position for a crash landing. The pilot is always in charge even if the co-pilot outranks him. To this day, I have never questioned his call.

Knowing we were going to crash and thinking there would be no survivors, I really prayed. First, I prayed for a comforter; I was no longer afraid of certain death. I prayed that my wife would live a long, happy life. I prayed that Mama and my family would be all right when they got the news. I was thankful that my brothers and their families would not have to go through this.

But, back to the crash . . .

Our crashed plane. Notice the open escape hatch at the top.

Another Plane Crash Photo

THE CRASH

We "landed," hitting an embankment on a dirt road. The underbelly of the plane was demolished. This, more than likely, kept us from rolling down a steep, 40- to 45-degree, hill. The plane came to a halt almost immediately.

Fire is always a major concern in any crash. The pilot's and co-pilot's escape hatch was directly overhead. We unlatched it and were out immediately. When we crashed, I hit my head on the instrument panel. I knew there was a cut on my forehead, so I leaned to the right to keep blood from getting on my face and in my eye. When I got nerve enough to check it, there was not even a scratch – just a small bruise! Someone was watching out for me.

The other hatch above the crew's crash position was always open. Two crew members were out and had moved away from the plane. The other two were injured and unable to get out on their own. I reached in and lifted one out by his parachute straps. He struggled to join the others that had escaped. I lifted the last crew member out by his parachute straps and tried to make him comfortable on the wing of the plane. We stayed there until help arrived.

An infantry unit had seen the crash and dispatched their medics to offer help. The two crew members who were injured, one with a neck injury and one with his back injured, were taken to where they could get proper treatment.

While all of this was happening, a French lady (an angel, I believe) brought two hot pies, one apple and one cherry, and placed them on the wing of the plane. I saw no house or any other structure nearby, nor did I see where she came from or where she returned to. The pies were a divine delicacy. I should know because I was the only one to eat them!

The infantry furnished us with transportation, food, and a place to stay. We were with them for two days. They had no way for us to communicate with our home base, so we were assigned a Jeep and a driver and told where we might find a phone.

Now, in those days, the military was still segregated. Only the officers were Caucasian. Our driver was a black sergeant. We started out to find Marsh, France. Every time we slowed down, an enlisted man asked if he could go with us. In a very short time, the jeep was loaded – not one more person could possibly get on. We found a phone, made the phone call to our base, and headed back to the ground unit.

On our return to the ground unit, they could not believe we had traveled as far as we had until a lieutenant explained how fast that "nigger sergeant" drove. We talked, had dinner, and talked some more about the war from the ground and air. Conversation got around to my pistol, an Army 45. One officer had always wanted one. I wanted a German Luger or a P-38. I gave him my 45. In the morning, he was going to take a metal detector and get me a pistol from the battlefield next to their camp. But, in the morning, we had transportation back to the airfield. He had my 45, but we couldn't wait for him to find a P-38. I left empty-handed.

Ed in snowy Cambrai

Back at the base, the other five crew members had left for a week of flak leave at Cannes, France. I had very little to do this week with no flying or other duties. As the crew was returning, I was on my way to Cannes.

While on leave, you were able to do whatever you wanted. Picture this. I even saw a high-ranking officer, a colonel, wearing a polka-dot shirt! I chose to stay in uniform all the time. Some of my time was spent in a lounge chair watching and listening to the big guns of war. We were close enough to the front lines to see and hear but were not in

Castle on the Riviera

any danger. Sightseeing from a bicycle was another pastime I enjoyed even though I wrecked once. While coasting down a hill, I put on the front brakes but not the rear ones. The front wheel stopped, but the back wheel and I kept going. Fortunately, the only thing hurt was my pride – a bomber pilot crash-lands a bicycle.

Cannes on the French Riviera

The sea and hotels were separated by a six- or seven-foot wall. Once, while walking on top of the wall gazing at the Mediterranean Sea and all the sun-bathers, I stepped off the wall. Again, the only thing hurt was my pride – a bomber pilot can't walk and chew gum at the same time. After a week of this "dangerous" assignment, it was back at the base where it was safe.

585th Bombardment Squadron (M) AAF

BACK TO WORK

Almost immediately we started flying missions again. By now, missions had become almost routine. The P-51s, English Spitfires, and a few P-38s were still giving us good cover when needed. The flak was heavy, but we had few losses from flak or enemy fighters.

On one mission, we were met by flak and ME-109 German fighters. This was not unusual. On the bomb

Arial Reconnaissance Photo

run, though, I looked to my right and saw something I had never seen or heard before. It was a German jet fighter. It came up under the flight and caused considerable damage but no loss of planes. Fortunately, he only had enough fuel to make one pass at the flight. We never saw a jet again on this or any other mission. We reported the jet at the debriefing. It was known that the Germans had jets, but we had not been told about them.

Ed with a tank

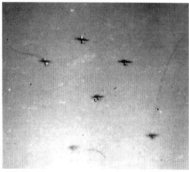

B-26 Formation

.Amos P. Potts Jr.. Edward J. Ryan

Lt. Amos P. Potts Jr., husband of Mrs. Marie R. Potts, 6206 Bedford Avenue, Fairfax, is now officer in charge of the Official Photo Mail Station at Paris, France.

Second Lt. Edward I. Ryon, husband of Mrs. Margaret Ryon, 128 West Nixon Street, Corryville, is serving as a B-26 Marauder pilot from a Ninth Air Force Bomber Base in France. He wears the Air Medal.

★ ★ ★

It was not uncommon to land a plane with holes in it from flak. Once, the tail gunner, Dick Hoyal, had the tube to his oxygen mask hit about six inches from his face. On that same mission a small piece of flak stopped in one of my boots. We had flak holes in our plane on many missions, but this was the only near miss.

When a mission started with limited visibility, it was almost always memorable. After takeoff, you would fly by instruments until you broke through and above the overcast. You knew the other planes in the squadron were close, but as hard as I tried (Rick was busy flying instruments), I could see nothing but solid clouds. It was always a concern that if you did see a plane, it would be too close for comfort.

When we finally saw blue sky, there were the other five planes just as if we were taking off. All six pilots had kept their air speed, rate of climb, and compass heading the same, just as they were supposed to. You could feel the collective sigh of relief. Our flight of six planes took our assigned position in the formation. We then, with the other flights, joined the squadron formation, and the lead plane set the heading for the target.

With our air speed over 200 mph and encountering a few bursts of inaccurate flak, we were soon over the target. The weather forecast had called for breaking clouds but it was not so. All we could see was solid overcast. So, we could not bomb this target. On missions like this, we usually had a secondary target. However, it was socked in too, so no bombs were dropped.

Each plane had two 2,000 pound bombs and nothing to do with them. We returned to the base and were glad to see the overcast breaking up. We waited our turn and came in to land. Rick set the plane down nice and easy and then "BAM" – a tire blew out. (If the bang had been a bomb, I wouldn't be writing about this mission!) Rick, ever so cool, kept the plane on the runway, slowed it down, and taxied off safely. I thanked God for yet another safe mission.

B-26 PILOT—Second Lt. Edward L. Ryon, pilot with a Ninth Air Force Marauder group in Europe, and son of James E. Ryon, Route 6, Chattanooga, is shown in the cockpit of his plane. He wears the Air Medal for meritorius achievement in aerial flight in Europe.

Our second and last flak leave was in Paris, France. The Allied forces had advanced a safe distance west of the city, so it was now safe for residents and visitors.

PARIS

On our arrival in Paris, we registered at our assigned hotel. We had comfortable rooms. Any room would be comfortable after life in tents and on cots. We were on our own for meals and entertainment. Neither one was hard to find. Rick and I spent most of our time together sightseeing. We found the Eiffel Tower, the Arc de Triomphe, and old cathedrals among other things.

Souvenir Photos from Paris

View from Central Hotel

Arc de Triomphe

Hotel in Paris

Hotel Card (to help you find your way back)

The evening meals were usually at a restaurant that had tables on the main floor and a balcony circling overhead with two stairways to the main floor and entrance.

Ed and Rick　　　　　Cathedral in Paris, France

We had finished our dinner. Rick had had a few more drinks than usual and was feeling gooooood. (In other words, he was drunk.) Halfway down the stairs, he got everyone's attention and told them what he had seen and what he wanted to see. (I won't go into detail here, so use your imagination.) We then made our way to the exit door and fresh air without further incident, thank heavens.

Usually, outside one of the places (joints), someone wanted you to see a "private" show downstairs. "Private show downstairs" was probably all the English the Parisian knew. I had heard about them and there was no way I was going to see one if I had been calling the shots. I just didn't know how Rick, in his condition, would feel about it. Thankfully, I didn't have to worry. He told them, "By the act of Congress, we are officers and gentlemen and we're not about to see any 'private' show." Thankfully again, after this incident we returned to the hotel and had a peaceful evening.

There was always excitement when out with Rick. One night we decided to go to another part of town. Why or where we were going, I do not remember. Rick could speak a little French, so he was the guide on this subway ride. Shortly after getting off the metro, we ran into two friends from the base. While the four of us were talking, two girls (well, there's another name for them) came walking toward us. Two MPs stepped up and informed us that if we were looking for girls, to just leave these two alone. I can't speak French, but there was no doubt about the "girls'" opinion of the MPs.

With two friends to look after Rick, I decided to head back to the hotel. What I needed, though, was someone to look out for me. On the subway, I couldn't remember where to get off or the name of the hotel. All I could do was guess. Fortunately, I guessed right. Otherwise, I could still be MIA (or AWOL?) in Paris. I was very happy that this was a successful "mission."

On another night, one of the crew members provided a little more excitement. He was about to kill a girl with a poker. The girl was pro-German and was talking bad about Americans. I heard a knock, rather a pound, on my door and was told all about it. Immediately, I was on my way (out of uniform) to try to help – that is, to try to calm things down. By the time I got there, though, all had quieted down and everyone lived. Each of us went to our rooms and headed back to the "safety" of the base the next morning.

THE REST OF THE WAR

By now, the war was beginning to slow down some. Or, at least we thought it was. In December of 1944, the Nazis made a massive offensive move – the Battle of the Bulge. We were told this was the first time the Germans had broken through our lines. This had us all worried. We were now back into some of the fiercest combat I had seen.

We were told to be concerned about two things: (1) they (the Germans) may sabotage our planes, and, (2) they would be hungry and may try to break into our mess halls. So, we posted guards at our planes and one at the mess hall at night. Everyone was given the password. One night, the cook returned to the mess hall for something he had forgotten. He was challenged by the guard. He had forgotten the password so he shouted out, "Don't shoot! It's Gonzales, de cooook!" That became our new password!

Due to a heavy overcast, the ground troops had very little support from us for the first part of the offensive.

New Suits of Armor Protect Air Crews

LONDON, Jan. 18 (AP).— American airmen are now almost entirely encased in armor when making missions over Germany. The new flak suit has specially-hardened steel in the back and front. Previously there was heavy metal only on the backing of plane seats.

Casualties from flak have been reduced by 66 percent by the armor suits. the Air Service Command reports.

Bombs Away! Sixteen 200 lb. Bombs, France, February 1945

While on the ground, there were plenty of air raid alerts. "December 20, 1944. Air raid alerts and paratroopers reported in vicinity. Germans strafing Cambrai – several killed."[6.]

When the weather cleared, we started flying every day. On some days, we flew several missions. On Christmas Day, our crew flew two missions. "December 25, 1944. A.M. – Bridge far in Germany. Milk run. Very successful. P.M. – St. With, Belgium marshalling yard." [6.]

On my birthday, March 11, we also gave ground support to the troops by flying two missions. "March 11, 1945. Hit an air field in the A.M. in Dulenberg, Germany and a marshalling yard in the P.M. MILK RUNS! Not a burst of flak. Short missions too. Near Dursburg, Germany." [6.] There were other two-mission days, but I particularly remember these two special occasions. Flak was usually intense on these missions. But we managed to hit our targets and return with little damage.

On Valentine's Day, one crew had trouble. Three were killed and one was hospitalized. "On February 21st, our group was attacked by fighters for the first time. We had lots of flak because of poor navigation through the fighters. It was a horrible sight. We lost some swell guys. We lost Ampolous. Also the crews of Hale, Coleman, and Abbott. Hale bailed out, Coleman crash landed, and Abbott may have landed. There were lots of empty sacks. Sure miss the guys that went down. They may be safe. Hope so." [6.]

On this mission, our plane was #2 in the flight position. We would fly off the left wing and slightly higher

[6.] Rubens, Alan I. *Personal War Diary*

'Clear Weather'—And the Air Force at Work

Objective: "To isolate enemy units from their supply sources." Result: the scenes above, showing two B26s of the Ninth Air Force dropping their bombs (top) and scoring direct hits (right) on the Konz-Karthaus railway bridge, a vital funnel for troop movements to Nazi forces.

U.S. Air Force Photos.

than the lead plane. From this position, it was easier for the co-pilot to see and stay in formation, so I flew most of this mission. All I saw was the lead plane and a few fighters that passed close to the formation. After the bomb run and the bombs dropped, we headed home. The lead planes' speed was increasing and the formation was getting loose. The wing man doesn't notice this; they just fly their position. Rick noticed the speed and wanted to slow down. But as long as a fighter was close, I was going to stay in formation. We made it back safely and I was more than glad to relax and let Rick, the pilot, take over the controls and land.

Again using Al Ruben's words to describe the situation, "On February 25th, two planes crashed in mid-air while getting into formation. All but one man was lost.

Close up of Martin B-26. (http://commons.wikimedia.org/wiki/Image:01097628_035.)

Aerial reconnaissance photo with dust and smoke showing bomb strikes

The remaining members are getting fewer in number. Seems our crew is about the only one left intact." [7.]

"March 1, 1945. Saw my first crash landing at midnight. Landing gear would not drop. Nose wheel twisted. He made a honey of a landing, really a thrill with sparks flashing and him skidding down the runway. No one hurt." [7.] Al explains it so well. I would have said, "When he touched the runway, it looked like the belly of the plane and the runway were on fire."

"March 14, 1945. Schaafheim, Germany. Target – air field. Perfect visibility. Could have been a milk run but poor navigation brought flak." [7.]

These missions started the same as most of the others. Usually, we saw very few enemy fighters. Flak would start as soon as we got in range of the anti-aircraft guns. Black puffs of smoke would let you know you were close to enemy lines. These explosions would be to the right, left, or high. As long as they missed their target, us, it was good. The ones we didn't like to see were the ones at our altitude in front or behind of the formation because, with a small correction, we would become the center of their target. A turn of a few degrees left or right would get us out of trouble most of the time. When the explosion was under the plane, you could feel it. It was not unusual to see a few holes appear in the fuselage.

"April 8, 1945. Northeast of Hannover. Good accurate flak for 30 seconds. Scared plenty! Flew tail gunner for the first time since third mission. Briefing 6 a.m. Engine time 4 p.m. Mission 4 hr. 20 min." [7.]

[7.] Rubens, Alan I. *Personal War Diary*

Martin B-26C in flight
http://www.maxwell.af.mil/au/afhra/phptp_galleries/merhar/Photos/01097628_035.jpg

"April 9, 1945. Lehrte, Germany. 6 min. east. Oil dump near Hannover. Was a milk run but long. Engine time was 5 p.m. and landed at 10 p.m.! Had a blowout after we started taxiing in. Lucky! [8]

"April 11, 1945. Aschersleben, Germany. Marshalling yard. Damn far in. Made three runs but finally hit it. No flak. Took 4 ½ hrs. on the gas." [8]

"April 12, 1945. Kempten, Germany. Bad weather so turned back. Got credit." [8]

Around the first of May, 1945, we were scheduled to move to an airfield near Venlo, Holland. Most of that field was in Germany. It was an extremely large field and we were to share it with another bomb group, a bomb wing headquarters, and a pathfinder squadron. The field

---

[8] Rubens, Alan I. *Personal War Diary*

Ed, Baber, Rick, Capt. Brooks   Ed and Captain Brooks

once had permanent housing, but it was destroyed when the Nazis vacated it. The story goes that the German C.O. and his staff all faced the Nazi firing squad for burning all the buildings. All that was left were runways and taxi strips.

The advance echelon had their work cut out for them. They had just a few days to get ready for the remaining personnel. When we arrived, the captain and lieutenants in charge of our quarters had things ready for us. We had a tent (which would be our living quarters until we left Europe) that was floored and had a stove for heat. Where they found the stoves, no one knows. Add a G.I. cot for sleeping and who could want anything more?

The "scuttlebutt" was that a peace treaty had been signed. Germany had surrendered!!! When the announcement was made on the 8th of May, the celebration really started. I don't believe the Dutch Guard or the 394th had an explosive of any kind that wasn't set off. Even the guns on the planes were fired until the barrels got red hot. As far as I know, no one was hurt. There were just a lot of headaches the next day from the noise and booze.

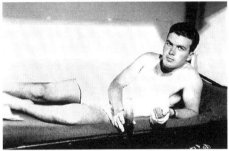

Ed posing in front of his tent, above, as a Pin-up model for Coca-Cola and Hersheys Chocolate, above right, and in his flight suit, right. Photos were taken in Venlo, Holland.

Ed posing with a cigar at the volleyball net

After a few days everything quieted down. We had very few assigned duties and did about anything we wanted to. We kept our flying time up. (We had to fly a certain number of hours to get flight pay.) We played volleyball for exercise.

One of the duties we officers had while serving in Europe was to censor mail. Although it was not a daily

Ed and Lew Kraft

task, we were expected to perform this duty as carefully as any other. It was considered necessary for our national security and for the success of our troops in the war.

A War Department pamphlet urged all of us, "THINK! Where does the enemy get his information – information that can put you, and has put your comrades, adrift on an open sea; information that has lost battles and can lose more, unless you personally, vigilantly, perform your duty

in SAFEGUARDING MILITARY INFORMATION?" [10.]
The pamphlet went on to list ten prohibited subjects.

In order to keep the censorship impersonal, I never saw a letter from any of my crew members. If I had, I would have passed the letter to someone else.

The one letter I do remember was from a sergeant to his mother. There was nothing to be censored, at least not about the war. It was just what he was saying to his mother that bothered me. After reviewing his letter, I asked that he report to me. When he did, I asked him to read the letter and tell me if he really wanted to mail it. He took one look at the letter and put it in his pocket and thanked me. As he was leaving, he turned again and said, "Thanks, Lieutenant, and I really mean it." I think I helped save one family the guilt and pain of words written in anger and frustration.

For some, gambling was their pastime. Most had a limit of two or three hundred dollars, but there were those who had no limits. I saw thousands (yes, thousands with an "s") bet on one roll of the dice. Headquarters got wind of the high-stakes games and stopped them. Too much money was being gambled and they were afraid someone might get hurt. My gambling consisted of penny poker. In a night, my winnings (or loss) would usually be less than a dollar. We could easily call that a pastime, not gambling.

More time was spent sightseeing than anything else. We would walk, ride bicycles, or ride motorcycles. Our only problem would be at the bridges crossing the rivers. Most of the bridges were bombed out by the "394th B.G." That was us. The Army had built new bridges. Most

---

[10.] War Department pamphlet No. 21-1, 29 July, 1943. See page 119

Captain Brooks Ed on Motorcycle Ed target shooting

of them were pontoon bridges and they kept them busy. The guards at the bridges didn't want us slowing down the convoys, so we had to find another way. We would go back four or five trucks to find one with room for us and our mode of transportation. We would ask if we could ride across. We were never refused. They even loaded our bicycles for us. I'm sure the guards and their officers knew what was going on. Their orders just didn't cover hitchhikers.

The destruction was hard to believe. We didn't have precision bombing back then, and a town would be completely destroyed just because it was close to an ammo dump, marshalling yard, or other target. If the town had been hit by artillery, there would only be holes in buildings, not the destruction caused by bombs. It was a shame what had to be done to bring the war in Europe to an end.

On our excursions, we were not expecting to see anything more than a few people, houses, or farm animals. However, we found a large factory. While we were at the gate and trying to figure out what kind of factory it was, a guard asked if we would like to come in and see the plant

Rick, Brooks. Ed

in operation. Even though we were in Holland, the guard was speaking a lot of French. Rick was speaking a little French. I was totally mute. As we entered, we saw that they were making cloth. (Do they make, spin, or weave cloth? I'll get out of this by saying it was a cloth factory.)

The tour was going fine but the conversation was completely in French. When I asked Rick what they were talking about, I found out it was that I worked with cloth back in the U.S. Since I "knew" so much about cloth, I thought I should act it out. Every roll we came to, I would look at it and feel it, then look up, nod and say "Good." I got a nod and a smile in return from our guide. As we entered the office, a man started speaking English with us about cloth goods. I was honest and explained to him I knew nothing about cloth. I just worked on the machines.

Ed alone, left, and Ed with his brother, Robert Ryon, in France

I've often wondered if he believed anything we said. After our "tour," we returned to the base for the evening meal.

We had some time to travel too. I knew my brother, Robert, was in France, so I contacted the Red Cross to find out where he was stationed. I then made arrangements to leave Venlo and go to France for a short visit. I had one day with Robert. We talked and ate at the mess hall. After that, it was back to Venlo. But it was a great day for both of us.

While we were stationed in Venlo, one of our many trips was to Brussels. It was a nice clean city and had lots to see. Most of our visits were spent sightseeing and taking pictures.

It wasn't long before orders started coming in for crews to return to the States. I had flown 46 ½ missions in combat and had received the Air Medal and eight oak leaf clusters for my service. I was ready to go home.

A special fountain in Brussells

Ed in Brussels

Post cards from Brussells:

Fiftieth Jubilee Arcade

Our Lady of Victory Church

Mionnaie Royal Theatre

Hal's Gate

GOING HOME, SWEET HOME

When our orders were finally posted, it didn't take us long to get ready. It was the old routine – put our belongings in a duffel bag, pull the drawstring, and wait.

The first leg of our trip was by train to Paris. It was crowded, hot, and had windows with no glass in them. We didn't care. We were headed home! The only stop I remember was short. We didn't even have time to get off and stretch. Even though we were told not to drink their water, some men asked bystanders for water. They were sick for the rest of the train ride.

A C-47 was our next mode of transportation. It had jump seats and was crowded too. There were no meals (not even peanuts!), no music, no air-conditioning, and certainly no flight attendant. We didn't care. We were headed home!

We flew the southern route going to Europe. We were taking the northern route home. The first stop was Iceland. We were to spend the night and fly out the next morning.

At breakfast, things looked bad – not the food – the weather. The airfield was completely closed, nothing in or

> **Baer, Arnold, Ryon May Get Discharge**
>
> Three Chattanooga combat airmen have returned from Europe and have reported to San Antonio, Tex., for reassignment or separation, according to an army release from the distribution command there.
> They are First Lt. Thomas Neal Baer, 1408 Bailey Avenue, B-17 pilot, captured in Italy when his plane was shot down on his 16th mission; First Lt. John A. Arnold, Route 1, P-47 pilot, with 180 combat hours, credited with two destroyed and two damaged enemy fighters, and First Lt. Edward L. Ryon, Route 6, B-26 pilot, holder of the Air Medal with eight clusters for 46 missions with the Ninth AAF.

```
                        R E S T R I C T E D
                            HEADQUARTERS
                       9TH BOMBARDMENT DIVISION (M)

                                              APO 140, U S Army,
                                              14 February 1945.
GENERAL ORDERS )
               :
NO . . . 22    )

                            E X T R A C T
           SECTION  V  :  AWARDS TO THE 394TH BOMBARDMENT GROUP (M).

                            SECTION     V

         By direction of the President, under the provisions of Executive
Order No. 9158, (Bull. 25, WD, 1942), as amended by Executive Order No.
9242-A, (Bull. 49, WD, 1942), and in accordance with authority delegated
by the War Department and contained in ETOUSA Circular #56, dated 27 May
1944, AIR MEDALS are awarded to the following named officers and enlisted
men of the 394th Bombardment Group (M), in recognition of meritorious
achievement while participating in aerial flights in the European Theater
of Operations, they each having completed the required number of operational
sorties against the enemy.
      *       *       *       *       *       *       *

                       585th Bombardment Squadron (M)


Edward L Ryon       0926376       2nd Lt      AC       Chattanooga, Tenn.

      *       *       *       *       *       *       *

              By command of Major General ANDERSON:

                                         RICHARD C SANDERS,
                                         Brig Gen, U S A,
                                         Chief of Staff.
OFFICIAL:

         s/C. C. Vega, Jr.,
         t/C. C. VEGA, JR.,
           Lt. Col., A. C.,
           Adjutant General.


                                       "A TRUE EXTRACT COPY"

                                       BEN H GOLDEN,
                                       1st Lt., A.C.,
                                       Asst. Adjutant.


                        R E S T R I C T E D
```

Ed was awarded the Air Medal in this letter dated February 14, 1945

out. It was this way for three or four weeks. We watched movies, played ping-pong, played pool (I'm definitely not a pool shark!), read, talked, and watched the weather.

> RESTRICTED
>
> HEADQUARTERS
> 9TH BOMBARDMENT DIVISION (M)
>
> GENERAL ORDERS) APO 140, U S Army,
> NO .... 38)   15 March 1945.
>
> EXTRACT
>
> SECTION II: AWARDS TO THE 394TH BOMBARDMENT GROUP (M).
>
> SECTION II
>
> By direction of the President, in addition to the Air Medals awarded in General Orders indicated by sub-paragraphs, the following named officers and enlisted men of the 394th Bombardment Group (M), are awarded the **first BRONZE OAK LEAF CLUSTER**, under the provisions of Executive Order No. 9158, (Bull. 25, WD, 1942), as amended by Executive Order No. 9242-A, (Bull. 49, WD, 1942), and in accordance with authority delegated by the War Department and contained in ETOUSA Circular #56, dated 27 May 1944, in recognition of meritorious achievement while participating in aerial flights in the European Theater of Operations, they each having completed the required number of operational sorties against the enemy.
>
> c. GO 22, Hq, 9th Bombardment Division (M) 14 Feb 1945.
>
> 585th Bombardment Squadron (M)
>
> Edward L Ryon   O-926376   2nd Lt   AC   Chattanooga, Tenn.
>
> By command of Major General ANDERSON:
>
>   RICHARD C SANDERS,
>   Brig. Gen, U S A,
> OFFICIAL: Chief of Staff.
>
> /s/ C. C. Vega, Jr.
> /t/ C. C. VEGA, JR.,
>   Lt. Col., A.C.,
>   Adjutant General.
>
>   "A TRUE EXTRACT COPY"
>
>   BEN H. GOLDEN,
>   1st Lt., A.C.,
>   Asst Adjutant.
>
> RESTRICTED

Ed was awarded eight Oak Leaf Clusters in addition to the Air Medal. (See pages 99 and 118.)

When the clouds lifted a couple hundred feet, you could barely see a small village to the northeast. We then understood why the air base was so well-equipped with good food and indoor activities. Anxious to get home, we knew the weather had to clear up sometime. It finally did and the airfield finally opened up. The C-47 lifted off and landed in Connecticut. It was the best landing a plane has ever made! Back on U.S. soil!

The stay at the air base in Connecticut was short, just long enough to get orders for our next assignment. We were given a few days leave, and then we were to report to San Antonio.

After buying a ticket, I boarded a fast bus to Cincinnati. Margaret was waiting for me as I stepped off the bus. She was prettier and sweeter than when I left her in Savannah a few months earlier. We had a few glorious days together. Too soon, it was time to say goodbye again. With a hug and a kiss, I was headed to Texas.

The photos above were the first pictures Margaret and I had made after my return from Europe. The dress Margaret is wearing was made from the silk fabric I had sent to her from Natal, Brazil. A lady in Cincinnati made it, another dress, and gowns with bed jackets to match, all from that silk. It was a beautiful dress and Margaret surprised me by wearing it to meet me at the bus station in Cincinnati. In the photo I have on the dress uniform I wore when we were married. Another wonderful memory.

The base in San Antonio was large and crowded. We were expecting orders to report somewhere in the South Pacific. But after Japan was bombed, we were hoping for a discharge. Things were moving slowly, too slowly for us. Very few were getting orders or discharges. Finally, the request came for volunteers to go to North Carolina to be discharged. This is the only time I volunteered for anything.

The train ride to Greensboro, North Carolina, was another long ride but, expecting a quick discharge, we didn't mind. We were going home! After unpacking and settling in, we had (and needed) some spare time.

I was unable to log any flying time in my travels from France to Greensboro. I needed to log a few hours to receive flight pay. The base only had small Stinson L-5 planes. I was asked, "Lieutenant, can you fly this L-5?" "Sure I can!" was my reply. After all, I had been flying planes for years.

On the flight line, I made all the pre-flight tests and got aboard. After starting the engine and checking the instruments and engine, I asked the tower for clearance to taxi for takeoff. Before getting on the runway, I advanced the throttle and checked the instruments one more time. The tower cleared me for takeoff. I taxied on to the runway, advanced the throttle to reach air speed, pulled slightly on the stick and I was airborne. It was good to be flying after two months on the ground. After clearing the traffic pattern, I was free to do whatever I wanted. I spent two hours looking at Greensboro, the farms, and the scenery. I then thought it was time to call it quits for the day, so I contacted the tower for landing instructions.

I entered the traffic pattern on the downwind leg, made the left turn on the base leg, and another left turn for the approach. All was going well. I was lined up with the runway. Over the runway, I tried to set the plane down, but when I pulled back on the controls to flare, the plane gained altitude. Too much air speed. The only thing to do was to advance the throttle and try one more time. The second attempt was the same as the first.

The tower was enjoying this way too much. I had to get this flight over with. The third time was a charm but not charming. Over the runway, the landing gear wheels gently made contact with the runway. Very little pressure on the controls and the plane stayed on the runway. I backed off the throttle. The plane lost air speed and the tail wheel settled on the runway. It was not a three-point landing (where all the wheels touch down at the same time) but it was safe and, by that time, that was all that mattered. The plane was taxied to the tarmac and tied down until the next day.

Still, I needed more flying time. The following day I was in the air again. Most of the time, three hours and fifteen minutes, was spent the same as the previous day, sightseeing from the air. The only change I made was practicing stalls. I had logged enough time for flight pay, so I contacted the tower for clearance to land. One more time, I was over the runway ready to set the plane down. I decreased the throttle, losing air speed, raised the nose, and stalled as the three wheels touched the runway. It was a perfect landing. This was my last flight for the United States Army Air Force. All I needed now was a discharge.

DISCHARGED

My discharge came through a few days later but was dated six weeks later. I had six weeks of accrued leave. When my leave was over, I would be out of the service. Or so I thought. For months after that, I received notices that I was subject to recall at any time. I was thankful that notices were all I ever received.

With a discharge in hand, I left Greensboro for Cincinnati. Margaret and I spent several pleasant days visiting with her family and friends. Our next stop was Chattanooga, Tennessee.

We stayed with Mom and Dad for a very short while until we bought a small house on South Concord Road. It had four rooms and one bathroom and sat on three acres not far from where we both grew up. The house and yard needed improvements, so we worked on that until we were able to move in. There were still lots of things that needed to be done so we stayed busy for a while.

Our first house

With moving and our first home improvements, I had done nothing about finding work. It was time to start looking. I put in applications at the airport and the telephone company. I accepted employment and was working for Southern Bell while still on leave from the USAAF. In

Discharge letter

a few days, the date on my discharge and the date on the calendar, (November 4, 1945) matched, so I was officially out of the Air Force. I started college at the University of Chattanooga at night. After two years, we started our

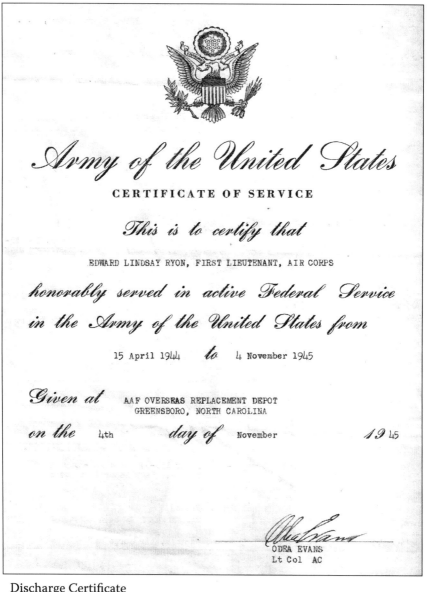

Discharge Certificate

family. The horrors, tears and fears, and sleepless nights of war were behind us. A beautiful life was before us.

The thirty-three months I was in the service were one of the highlights of my life, especially after Margaret and I were married. We both liked military service except for one thing. We didn't want to move every two or three years. We needed a permanent base. It was home sweet home for us. With God's blessing, we planted strong roots and have been in Chattanooga ever since.

THE REUNION

I was fortunate enough to be able to fly with the same crew on all forty-six of my missions except the one mentioned earlier in the book. It was truly a miracle. After the war ended, each crew member said their goodbyes. It was sad but wonderful that we all were headed home to start a new and different life. As we left Venlo, Holland, we just assumed we would stay in touch. Unfortunately, and unbelievably, it didn't happen.

Fifty years after Margaret and I had exhausted our search for the other crew members, we had a phone call from the airport in Chattanooga. In August, 1995, Al Ruben's son was making a business trip to Cleveland, Tennessee, a twenty-minute drive from Chattanooga. Al lived in Chicago. Almost on a whim, Al asked him to look in the Chattanooga phone directory and see if I was still in the area. His son did as he was asked and looked me up. He gave me a call and we talked a long time. Truly another miracle had happened.

Our 50 Year Reunion in Janesville, Wisconsin. Front row: Lew Kraft, Dick Hoyal, Margaret Ryon and Ed. Second row: Donna Kraft, Elaine Rubens, and Al Rubens.

Al's son gave me his dad's phone number and address. It only took me a minute (if that long!) to call Al. We were so excited we could hardly speak. The emotion was more than my words can describe. From that call, things started to happen.

Several days later, Al called and told us they were moving to another house in Chicago, and he and his wife were going through boxes and boxes of things they had stored for years in their attic. In the top of the first box they opened, was a holiday greeting card dated December 15, 1950, that we had sent to his mother's address with a note saying, "Hope to see you soon."

"Soon" was fifty years later. Al knew where all the crew members lived. Sadly, two had died several years earlier. The other two members lived in Dixon, Illinois, and in Wisconsin.

It only took about two weeks for Al and his wife (Elaine) to get everything organized for a reunion. We

Ed Ryon, Lew Kraft, Dick Hoyal, Al Rubens

met in Janesville, Wisconsin, in September of 1995. I can never explain the joy and emotion that was shared that day. Everyone was talking at one time. We had to restrain ourselves and enjoy the moment. This was a new beginning. The crew swapped tales.

I had to let the guys in on a couple of secrets I had kept all these years. After bombing missions, the officers were treated to whiskey. The enlisted men were not as fortunate. Since I didn't drink, I would tell the bartender to give mine to the enlisted men once I had accumulated a fifth. They never knew where the whiskey came from until fifty years later. We had a laugh over that one. I also told Al Rubens about my prayers and concerns for him during the war. As Al was Jewish, I feared for his life if he were ever captured by the Nazis. He was so touched. Later he wrote me and told me that all of Chicago knew who I was, as he had told them of my prayers.

One night as we were having dinner (and again we were all talking non-stop), Margaret noticed that a couple sitting near our table had been served their dinner but they were not eating. They just sat watching and listening to our group telling their stories of their missions together. They never finished their dinner. As they were leaving, Margaret spoke to them and apologized for disturbing their dinner. They just said, "Thank you for letting us share in all your stories."

What a wonderful three days and nights together! They passed too quickly. As we were saying our good-byes again fifty years later, tears were in our eyes, and we promised never to lose contact again. We kept our promise this time.

At each reunion, we continued to laugh and cry as we reminisced and recounted our adventures. We met again in September, 1996, in Minneapolis, Minnesota. It was a joyous reunion once again.

There was another reunion in Florida in 1997, but we did not get to attend due to health reasons. Sadly, after that, Al's wife Elaine had passed away, as had Lew Kraft, the bombardier. The last reunion was here in Chattanooga and only Margaret and I attended.

Age has taken its toll on us. Even with all the "distractions" that happen in the "golden" years, both Dick and Al visited us here in the "good ol' South." Dick Hoyal died in March, 2007. Now Al and I are all who remain of the crew of six. We two crew members who are left have promised to keep in touch and to pray for peace for all people.

Even as I reminisce now, I am reminded again about how good my God has been to me.

AFTERWORD

True to our commitment and "base," Margaret and I have been married over sixty-three years. As we had our two children, we soon outgrew our house on Concord Road and moved a short distance to a larger house on Igou Gap Road. We have been there for fifty-three years.

It is called a "memory house" for us as well as our children, grandchildren, and, hopefully, our great-grandchildren. I hope this book adds to those memories. It has truly been home sweet home for all of our family. We have loved our years together and look forward to more years with family and friends.

Keep love in your heart, for our God is a God of love.

LOVE,

Ed/Dad/Papa

Our "Memory House" in Chattanooga, Tennessee

1ST LT. ED RYON'S MISSIONS

Date	Aircraft Type & Model	Duty	Mission	Combat Time	Sortie No.
19-Nov-44	B-26G5	CP	Bomb	3:00	1
10-Dec-44	B-26F1	CP	Bomb	2:15	2
13-Dec-44	B-26F1	CP	Bomb	2:50	3
23-Dec-44	B-26C45	CP	Bomb	3:00	4
24-Dec-44	B-26C45	CP	Bomb	2:50	5
25-Dec-44	B-26G15	CP	Bomb	3:20	6
25-Dec-44	B-26G1	CP	Bomb	2:50	7
27-Dec-44	B-26C45	CP	Bomb	3:05	8
6-Jan-45	B-26G15	CP	Bomb	2:50	9
29-Jan-45	B-26B55	CP	Bomb	3:30	10
6-Feb-45	B-26G1	CP	Bomb	4:30	11
9-Feb-45	B-26G1	CP	Bomb	3:00	12
10-Feb-45	B-26G1	CP	Bomb	2:30	13
16-Feb-45	B-26B55	CP	Bomb	5:15	14
19-Feb-45	B-26B55	CP	Bomb	3:30	15
21-Feb-45	B-26G1	CP	Bomb	4:10	16
24-Feb-45	B-26G15	CP	Bomb	2:40	17
24-Feb-45	B-26G5	CP	Bomb	2:10	18
28-Feb-45	B-26G20	CP	Bomb	3:00	19
1-Mar-45	B-26F1	CP	Bomb	3:50	20
2-Mar-45	B-26G20	CP	Bomb	4:15	21

3-Mar-45	B-26G5	CP	Bomb	2:45	22
6-Mar-45	B-26G20	CP	Bomb	4:00	23
11-Mar-45	B-26G15	CP	Bomb	3:50	24
11-Mar-45	B-26G15	CP	Bomb	4:00	25
12-Mar-45	B-26G5	CP	Bomb	3:15	26
13-Mar-45	B-26F1	CP	Bomb	3:30	27
14-Mar-45	B-26G5	CP	Bomb	3:45	28
15-Mar-45	B-26G15	CP	Bomb	2:40	29
17-Mar-45	B-26G25	CP	Bomb	3:40	30
17-Mar-45	B-26G5	CP	Bomb	3:45	31
18-Mar-45	B-26G20	CP	Bomb	3:35	32
18-Mar-45	B-26G15	CP	Bomb	3:20	33
22-Mar-45	B-26G5	CP	Bomb	3:25	34
23-Mar-45	B-26G10	CP	Bomb	2:40	35
24-Mar-45	B-26G10	CP	Bomb	3:10	36
25-Mar-45	B-26G15	CP	Bomb	3:00	37
6-Apr-45	B-26G10	CP	Bomb	3:00	38
8-Apr-45	B-26G1	CP	Bomb	4:30	39
9-Apr-45	B-26G25	CP	Bomb	5:10	40
11-Apr-45	B-26G15	CP	Bomb	5:30	41
12-Apr-45	B-26G20	CP	Bomb	3:50	42
14-Apr-45	B-26G20	CP	Bomb	2:30	43
15-Apr-45	B-26G20	CP	Bomb	4:30	44
17-Apr-45	B-26G20	CP	Bomb	5:05	45
19-Apr-45	B-26G1	CP	Bomb	4:40	46

MISCELLANEOUS PHOTOS/ DOCUMENTS

UNITED STATES OF AMERICA
DEPARTMENT OF COMMERCE
CIVIL AERONAUTICS ADMINISTRATION
WASHINGTON

Form ACA 348 (Rev. 1-1-45)

AIRMAN CERTIFICATE NO. **97450**

This certifies that EDWARD LINDSAY RYON has been found to be properly qualified to exercise the privileges of A PILOT

Address ROUTE #6, CHATTANOOGA, TENNESSEE

SEX	DATE OF BIRTH	WEIGHT	HEIGHT	HAIR	EYES
MALE	3-11-23	185	6'	BROWN	HAZEL

THIS CERTIFICATE is of such duration as is provided in currently effective Civil Air Regulations.

Date of Issuance OCTOBER 5, 1945

By direction of the Administrator

M. D. GIRTON
Civil Aeronautics Inspector

This certificate is not valid unless accompanied by a Medical Certificate evidencing compliance with the pertinent physical requirements, an appropriate Rating Record when required bearing the above number, and other evidence as required under the currently effective Civil Air Regulations. Any alteration of this certificate is punishable by a fine of not exceeding $1,000 or imprisonment not exceeding three years, or both.

(er) Signature of Holder

Airman Certificate

394th BOMB GROUP (M)

584th, 585th, 586th, 587th
BOMBARDMENT SQUADRONS

ACTIVATED - 15 FEBRUARY 1943
DEACTIVATED - 15 FEBRUARY 1946

DEDICATED TO ALL THE MEN WHO SERVED IN THE 394th BOMB GROUP.

24 JULY 1989

Monument at Air Force Museum

HEADQUARTERS
ARMY AIR FORCES GULF COAST TRAINING CENTER
Office of the Commanding General

August 7, 1943   Randolph Field, Texas

Mr. and Mrs. James C. Ryon, Sr.,
Rt. #6,
Chattanooga, Tenn.

Dear Mr. and Mrs. Ryon:

       In a memorandum which has come to my desk this morning, I note that your boy has been classified for Pilot training and that he is being appointed an Aviation Cadet in the Army Air Forces.

       In order to win this war, it is vital to have the best qualified young men at the controls of our military aircraft. Upon their precision, daring and coolness will depend in large measure the success of our entire war effort.

       The duties of an Army Pilot call for a high degree of mental and physical alertness, sound judgment, and an inherent aptitude for flying. Men who will make good material for training as Pilots are rare. The Classification Board believes your boy is one of them and that he will in all probability win his wings as a military pilot.

       You must realize, however, that all of our study of the problem has produced no infallible method of determining in advance whether a young man has that inherent something which will make him a natural and safe pilot. As a result, some pilot candidates are later transferred to other types of military training.

       Comprehensive tests indicate that your boy stands a very good chance of successfully completing the rigid training for an army pilot and you have every reason to be proud of him. I congratulate you and him.

                                                 Sincerely yours,

                                                G. C. BRANT
                                            Major General, U.S. Army
                                                   Commanding

Letter to Ed's parents saying he has earned Aviation Cadet status

```
                HEADQUARTERS OF THE ARMY AIR FORCES
                              WASHINGTON

                                              9 September 1944

      PERSONNEL ORDERS)
      NO.       217  )

                              EXTRACT

          16. The following-named Second Lieutenants, Air Corps (AUS),
      are rated Pilot, under the provisions of Army Regulations 95-60,
      War Department, 1942, and paragraph 3 c, Army Air Forces Regu-
      lation 50-7, dated 1 June 1944, effective 10 September 1944:

                   Roger Thomas Barnes, 0-926390
                   Joseph Brudnicki, 0-926437
                   Robert Henry Cunliffe, 0-926431
                   Jack Gorman McGhee, 0-926432
                   Adam Milton Ranck, 0-926374
                   Harvey Paul Roland, 0-926375
                   Edward Lindsay Ryon, 0-926376

          17. Pursuant to authority contained in paragraph 2, sub-
      paragraph 2, Army Regulations 35-1480, dated 10 October 1942,
      the following-named Second Lieutenants, Air Corps (AUS), each
      of whom holds an aeronautical rating, are hereby required to
      participate in regular and frequent aerial flights:

                   Roger Thomas Barnes, 0-926390
                   Joseph Brudnicki, 0-926437
                   Robert Henry Cunliffe, 0-926431
                   Jack Gorman McGhee, 0-926432
                   Adam Milton Ranck, 0-926374
                   Harvey Paul Roland, 0-926375
                   Edward Lindsay Ryon, 0-926376

               By command of General ARNOLD:

                                    J. M. BEVANS
                                    Major General, U.S. Army
                                    Assistant Chief of Air Staff,
                                    Personnel

              WALLS
           Major, Air Corps
           Chief, Flying Status Section
           Office of Asst. Chief of Air Staff,
           Personnel
```

Official rating as Pilot US Army Air Corps

This is when Page was made 1st Lt

RESTRICTED

HEADQUARTERS
NINTH AIR FORCE

APO 696, U S Army
9 April 1945

SPECIAL ORDERS)
:
NUMBER......99)   E X T R A C T
          *   *   *   *   *

15. DP, the fol named Officers are promoted to the temp gr indicated, in the AUS w/ rank from date of this order. Exceptional circumstances exist which sv the best interests of the sv. AUTH: Par 5d, AR 605-12 as amended, and Cir 90, Hq, European TO USA, 1944.

FIRST LIEUTENANT TO CAPTAIN
ROBERT A. TROMBETTA   0767420   AC   PATRICK B. TURNER   0697240   AC

SECOND LIEUTENANT TO FIRST LIEUTENANT

KENNETH C. GOWDY	0774123	AC	WILLIAM H. PALMER	0830298	AC
JAMES L. HASMAN	0830459	AC	STEPHEN L. PASCAL	0773791	AC
VERNON E. HIBBING	0759000	AC	GEORGE W. PATTERSON, JR.	0713597	AC
LEWIS J. HILL	0711206	AC	ROBERT H. PEDERSEN	0714157	AC
HAROLD W. RILLMAN	0720506	AC	DOUGLAS B. PERRY	0721854	AC
LAWRENCE M. HOHLAUS	0822439	AC	ROBERT W. PHILLIPS	0773797	AC
CHARLES L. HOLLIS, JR.	0721757	AC	DALE C. PRENTICE	0779218	AC
WILLIAM M. HOLMES	0697325	AC	WILLIAM F. REILLY	0761304	AC
JOHN T. HOPKINS, JR.	0715968	AC	EDWARD M. ROSENBERG	0765724	AC
JOHN L. HOST	0720381	AC	RAYMOND K. ROWLAND	0779227	AC
CHRISTIAN A. HOVDE	0716145	AC	★ EDWARD L. RYON	0926376	AC
FRANK A. JOHNSON	0720518	AC	JAMES R. SCALLY	0779230	AC
GEORGE G. JOHNSON	0749965	AC	FRANCIS A. SCHNEPPER	0719763	AC
JUNIE O. JOHNSON	0816111	AC	GLENN L. SCHRADER	0779234	AC
LLOYD W. JOHNSON	0823083	AC	FRED W. SCHULTZ	0778973	AC
HAROLD JOYCE	0722653	AC	CURTIS H. SCROGGINS	0779240	AC
ROBERT H. KEGARISE	0721115	AC	WILBUR E. SHAKRO	0715024	AC
CHARLES G. KELLEY	01995974	AC	SAMUEL J. SHOEMAKER	0765735	AC
FINIS M. KELLEY	0781592	AC	DALTON H. SHROYER	02059622	AC
ROBERT J. KETTERER	0765498	AC	DONALD M. SIAGLE	0779248	AC
FREDERICK N. KING	0832619	AC	ALVIN O. SMITH	0715819	AC
FRANK W. KINNEY	02056979	AC	HERBERT W. SMITH, JR.	0779731	AC
LEONARD KRIM	0780628	AC	RAYMOND R. SMITH	0718789	AC
JOHN M. LAFERTY, JR.	0720274	AC	JOHN SOMERS	0714206	AC
JOHN A. LAWRENCE	0708706	AC	JOHN W. SPIRES	0768364	AC
GEORGE B. LE FEVER, JR.	0557869	AC	ERNEST M. SPROUSE	0830568	AC
THORNE W. LONGSWORTH	0713822	AC	FENWICK STILLMAN	0759992	AC
THOMAS J. LOTINA, JR.	0713823	AC	WALTER R. ST PIERRE	0777836	AC
HUGH C. LUTERICK	0783199	AC	JAMES E. TEAL	0824776	AC
SIDNEY P. MANDERSON	0675510	AC	ARTHUR A. THOMPSON, JR	02068163	AC
EARL W. MAPLE	0760883	AC	MICHAEL A. TITRE	0770008	AC
RICHARD F. MC VEY	0714731	AC	RUSSELL H. TRAPPER	0741113	AC
WILBUR W. METCALF	0833372	AC	SIDNEY L. TUMPSON	0679259	AC
SHERWOOD B. MILLER	0831239	AC	JOHN D. VANDERMAY	0765453	AC
REUBEN J. MISSIMER	0713859	AC	GARRETT A. VEEDER	0816676	AC
DONALD E. MITCHELL	0830050	AC	HOWARD R. VIA	02061289	AC
FREDERICK W. MITCHELL, JR	0779192	AC	EDWARD L. WALKER	0824298	AC
HANFERD J. MOEN	0778899	AC	JOHN B. WALTERS	0719522	AC
BYRD R. MOORE, JR.	0773196	AC	GEORGE F. WEGMAN	0750495	AC
JOHN W. MORLEY	0773197	AC	LLOYD E. WEINBERG	0721271	AC
WILLIAM F. MORRIS, JR.	0779945	AC	JAMES E. WELDON	0778633	AC
BERNARD P. MOURA	0778537	AC	CHARLES A. WENTLAND	0722228	AC
RICHARD C. MUIR	0722521	AC	ROBERT K. YOUNG	0721893	AC

         *   *   *   *   *

By command of Major General VANDENBERG:

                                            W W MILLARD
                                            Colonel, GSC
OFFICIAL: *F. H. Monahan*   C of S

F. H. MONAHAN
Lt Col, A G D
Asst Adj Gen
DISTRIBUTION: "A"   -2-   R E S T R I C T E D

Appointment to First Lieutenant

```
                HEADQUARTERS 394TH BOMBARDMENT GROUP (M)
                       Office of the Group Commander

                                                    APO 140, U S Army
                                                    7 July       1945.

                              C E R T I F I C A T E

          This is to certify that   1st Lt  Edward L. Ryon    ASN 0-926376

      has participated in  46 ½  Bomber Sorties with the organization on dates indicated

         19 Nov 44            25 Feb 45            18 Mar 45
         10 Dec 44            28 Feb 45            22 Mar 45
         13 Dec 44             1 Mar 45            23 Mar 45
         23 Dec 44             2 Mar 45            24 Mar 45
         24 Dec 44             3 Mar 45            25 Mar 45
         25 Dec 44             6 Mar 45             6 Apr 45
         25 Dec 44            11 Mar 45             8 Apr 45
         27 Dec 44            11 Mar 45             9 Apr 45
          6 Jan 45            12 Mar 45            11 Apr 45
          9 Feb 45            13 Mar 45            12 Apr 45
         10 Feb 45            14 Mar 45            14 Apr 45
         16 Feb 45            15 Mar 45            15 Apr 45
         19 Feb 45            17 Mar 45            17 Apr 45
         21 Feb 45            17 Mar 45            19 Apr 45
         24 Feb 45            18 Mar 45

      Individual concerned has been credited with  ½  additional missions for flying 2
      lead positions to complete a tour of  46 ½  missions.

      AWARDS:
      AIR MEDAL -    GO 22, 9th B Div, 14 Feb 45
      1st OLC to Air Medal - GO 38, 9th B. Div, 15 Mar 45.
      2nd OLC to Air Medal - GO 38, 9th B. Div, 15 Mar 45.
      3rd OLC to Air Medal - GO 58, 9th B. Div, 21 Apr 45.
      4th OLC to Air Medal - GO 69, 9th B. Div,  6 May 45.
      Silver or 5th OLC to Air Medal - GO 69, 9th B. Div, 6 May 45.
      6th OLC to Air Medal - GO 69, 9th B Div  6 May 45.
      7th OLC to Air Medal - GO  6, 9th A.D, 15 May 45.
      8th OLC to Air Medal - GO  6, 9th A.D, 15 May 45.
      9th OLC to Air Medal -
      2nd Silver or 10th OLC to Air Medal -




                  For the Group Commander:
                                                    H. Brickman, Maj. AC

                                                    BEN H. GOLDEN,
                                                    1st Lt., A.C.,
                                                    Asst Adjutant.
```

Total number of missions 46 ¹/2. Awards: One Air Medal, One Silver Oak Leaf Cluster, Seven Bronze Oak Leaf Clusters

War Department Pamphlet No. 21-1   29 July 1943

WHEN YOU ARE OVERSEAS

THESE FACTS ARE VITAL

Writing home

THINK! Where does the enemy get his information--information that can put you, and has put your comrades, adrift on an open sea; information that has lost battles and can lose more, unless you personally, vigilantly, perform your duty in SAFEGUARDING MILITARY INFORMATION?

CENSORSHIP RULES ARE SIMPLE, SENSIBLE.--They are merely concise statements drawn from actual experience briefly outlining the types of material which have proved to be disastrous when available to the enemy. A soldier should not hesitate to impose his own additional rules when he is considering writing of a subject not covered by present regulations. He also should guard against repeating rumors or misstatements. It is sometimes stated that censorship delays mail for long periods of time. Actually, mail is required to be completely through censorship within 48 hours.

There are ten prohibited subjects

1. Don't write military information of Army units--their location, strength, materiel, or equipment.
2. Don't write of military installations.
3. Don't write of transportation facilities.
4. Don't write of convoys, their routes, ports (including ports of embarkation and disembarkation), time en route, naval protection, or war incidents occurring en route.
5. Don't disclose movements of ships, naval or merchant, troops, or aircraft.
6. Don't mention plans and forecasts or orders for future operations, whether known or just your guess.
7. Don't write about the effects of enemy operations.
8. Don't tell of any casualty until released by proper authority (The Adjutant General) and then only by using the full name of the casualty.
9. Don't attempt to formulate or use a code system, cipher, or shorthand, or any other means to conceal the true meaning of your letter. Violations of this regulation will result in severe punishment.
10. Don't give your location in any way except as authorized by proper authority. Be sure nothing you write about discloses a more specific location than the one authorized.

INCLOSURES IN LETTERS.--Do not inclose anything in a letter that would violate any of the foregoing rules.

PHOTOGRAPHS, FILMS.--Special rules apply to the transmission of photographs and films. Do not send them until you have ascertained what regulations are in effect in your area.

540677--43

Rules for writing home

RÉPUBLIQUE FRANÇAISE

Guerre 1939-1945

CITATION

EXTRAIT DE LA DECISION N° 332

LE PRESIDENT DU GOUVERNEMENT PROVISOIRE DE LA REPUBLIQUE

CITE A L'ORDRE DE L'ARMEE

- 394th Bomb Group

"Magnifique unité de combat qui se distingua par sa valeur militaire, sa détermination, son endurance et son courage exceptionnel.

A joué un rôle important dans la victoire des Alliés par ses actions rapides et opportunes durant plus de 2500 missions, notamment entre le 6 juin et le 14 septembre 1944.

Immobilisa les renforts ennemis dirigés vers les plages normandes et précipita la défaite de l'ennemi par ses actions de soutien aux forces alliées terrestres traversant la France.

En moins de trois mois, détruisit 17 ponts, 17 dépôts d'essence, 9 fortifications et attaqua 5 concentrations de troupes, 4 dépôts protégés et d'autres cibles importantes.

Par la valeur et l'efficacité de ses bombardements, a largement contribué au succès des forces alliées de libération."

CETTE CITATION COMPORTE L'ATTRIBUTION DE LA CROIX DE GUERRE AVEC PALME.

Paris, le 17 septembre 1946
Signé : BIDAULT

EXTRAIT CERTIFIE CONFORME
Washington, le APR 19 1991
Pour le Ministre et par autorisation
l'Attaché de Défense à Washington

French Citation authorizing the *Croix de Guerre* for Ed's Bomb Group.

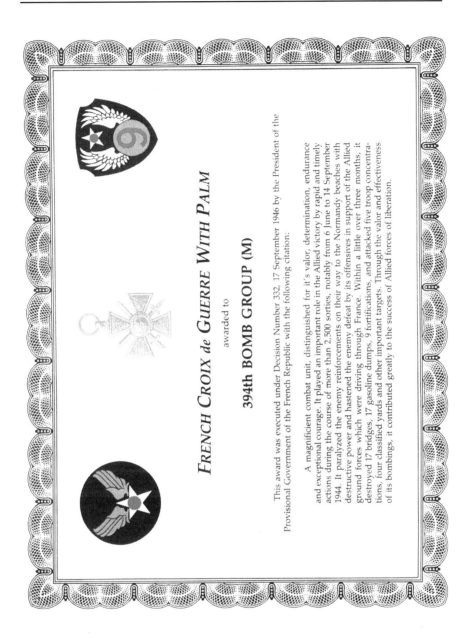

French *Crois de Guerre* (War Cross) With Palm

```
                    R E S T R I C T E D
                HEADQUARTERS 394TH BOMBARDMENT GROUP (M) AAF
                        Office of the Group Commander

                                                    APO 140, U S Army,
                                                    22  April  1945.
SPECIAL ORDERS )
NUMBER      69 )

    1. UP AR 605-115 and 9BD TWX P-1593-C, the foll named O, orgns as indicated
are hereby granted seven (7) days lv of abs (ord) eff o/a 23 April 1945, O will
report to 1st Lt JAMES BEERS, Liaison Officer, US Riveria Recreational Area,
Martinez Hotel, Cannes, France:

                1ST LT JOSEPH GALLEGOS    O 782 254    584th Bomb Sq (M)
                2D LT LAWRENCE E. KANTER  O2 062 215   584th Bomb Sq (M)
                1ST LT LEWIS E. KRAFT     O 723 754    585th Bomb Sq (M)
                2D LT EDWARD L. RYON      O 926 376    585th Bomb Sq (M)

    2. UP AR 615-5 and upon the recommendation of his orgn comdr Pvt Kazimierz
J. Olejarcyzk, 10 601 947 (509), 586th Bomb Sq (M), is hereby promoted to gr of
Sergeant (Temp).

        By order of Colonel CELIO:

                                                    HENRY G. BRICKMAN,
                                                    Major, Air Corps,
                                                    Adjutant.
OFFICIAL:

    Henry G. Brickman
    HENRY G. BRICKMAN,
    Major, Air Corps,
    Adjutant.

                    R E S T R I C T E D
```

Letter granting leave for Cannes, France

Patch of the Ninth Air Force

Army of the United States

SEPARATION QUALIFICATION RECORD
SAVE THIS FORM. IT WILL NOT BE REPLACED IF LOST

This record of job assignments and special training received in the Army is furnished to the soldier when he leaves the service. In its preparation, information is taken from available Army records and supplemented by personal interview. The information about civilian education and work experience is based on the individual's own statements. The veteran may present this document to former employers, prospective employers, representatives of schools or colleges, or use it in any other way that may prove beneficial to him.

1. LAST NAME—FIRST NAME—MIDDLE INITIAL			MILITARY OCCUPATIONAL ASSIGNMENTS		
RYON EDWARD LINDSAY			10. MONTHS	11. GRADE	12. MILITARY OCCUPATIONAL SPECIALTY
2. ARMY SERIAL NO.	3. GRADE	4. SOCIAL SECURITY NO.	19	1st Lt	1082 Pilot B-26
O 926 376	1st Lt				
5. PERMANENT MAILING ADDRESS (Street, City, County, State)					
Rt #6, Chattanooga, Tenn.					
6. DATE OF ENTRY INTO ACTIVE SERVICE	7. DATE OF SEPARATION	8. DATE OF BIRTH			
15 Apr 44	4 Nov 45	11 Mar 23			
9. PLACE OF SEPARATION					
AAF ORD Greensboro, N.C.					

SUMMARY OF MILITARY OCCUPATIONS

13. TITLE—DESCRIPTION—RELATED CIVILIAN OCCUPATION

Pilots aircraft and commands crew. Inspects aircraft prior to flight Must have thorough knowledge of flight navigation instruments, radio, meteorology, and operation of engines.

Qualified for flying jobs and those requiring manual dexterity and quick psychomotor reactions.

WD AGO FORM 100
1 JUL 1945
This form supersedes WD AGO Form 100, 15 July 1944, which will not be used.

Ed's official separation papers

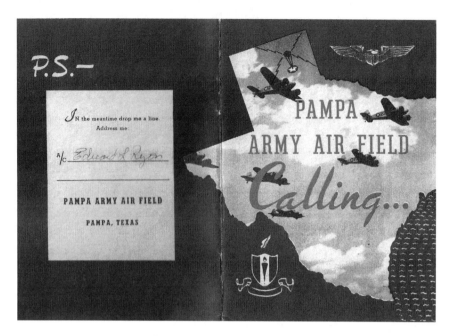

Taken from *Pampa Army Air Field Calling*

Taken from *Pampa Army Air Field Calling*

Taken from *Pampa Army Air Field Calling*

Taken from *Pampa Army Air Field Calling*

Taken from *Pampa Army Air Field Calling*

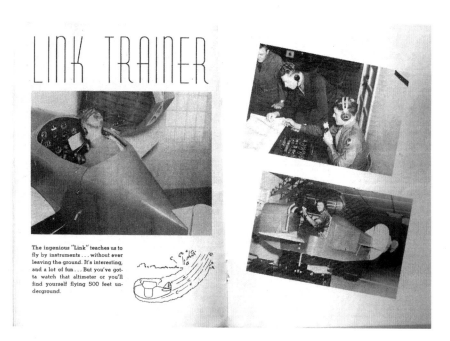

Taken from *Pampa Army Air Field Calling*

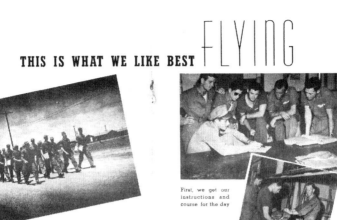

Taken from *Pampa Army Air Field Calling*

Taken from *Pampa Army Air Field Calling*

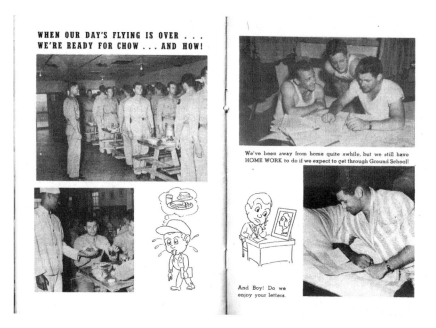

Taken from *Pampa Army Air Field Calling*

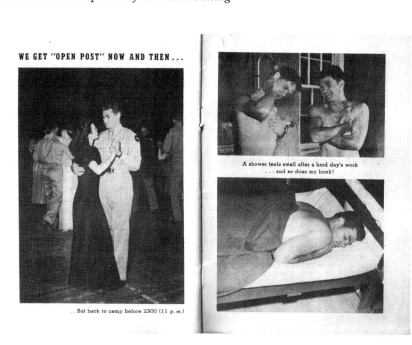

Taken from *Pampa Army Air Field Calling*

Taken from *Pampa Army Air Field Calling*

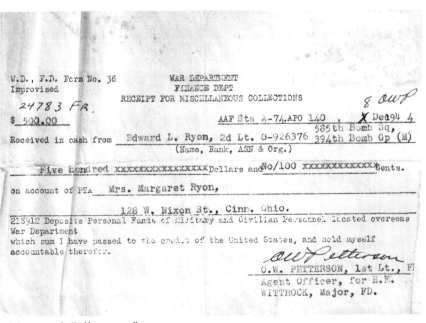

Margaret's "Allowance"

The Pampa Army Airfield "Yearbook"

N. ACUFF
Instructor

G. L. Ryon
Chattanooga, Tennessee

Morley K. Russell
1303 Pine
Texarkana, Texas

Clarence R. McConnaughey
422 N. Main Street
Lewisburg, Ohio

Harold J. Nanney
6203 Atoll Avenue
Van Nuys, California

Page from Gremlins, Hicks Field, Fort Worth, Texas, 44-D Yearbook

A. I. Rubens
485 Monroe Avenue
Glencoe, IL 60022

12-12-'95

Dear Ed-Margaret:

By now half of Chicago knows what old Ed Dyer looks like, I guess the other half don't care.

I too can't stop thinking about the thrill and excitement of seeing you all again after so many years. It seems incredable, words just can't describe how I feel. Of course the one thing that shakes me up is your concern for my well being if we got shot down, you're one helluva man!

You went on a river-boat at Thanksgiving, well I've established a tradition for years of taking my "nearest and dearest"

Portion of Letter from Al Rubens

War Diary of Alan I. Rubens
(reprinted by permission)

Note: The original diary was handwritten. In transcribing, some of the village names may be misspelled, but we did the best we could.

Date: September 10, 1944
Place: Hunter Field, GA
We were supposed to leave 72 hours after arrival. Things were mixed up and we left after 33 days of sack time.

Date: October 14, 1944
Place: Bolling Field, D.C.
Had a terrific time in Washington. Were processed and left from Nat'l Airport the 18th by AT-4 planes. C-54

Date: October 19, 1944
Place: Goose Bay, Labrador
First step from the U.S. A small ATC base between nowhere and nowhere else. Had chow and flew out after an hour. Pretty damn cold.

Date: October 19, 1944, 11:00 a.m.
Place: Meeks Field, Iceland
This really is rough stuff. Only a stop off for our plane. Damn cold here too. Saw all kinds of uniforms and heard a British radio broadcast. Left after an hour or so. Beginning to realize we are going across and they aren't jiving.

Date: October 20, 1944
Place: Adamton Field, Prestwick, Scotland
Arrived at 8 p.m. Now we are overseas. Changed our money into pounds and shillings (more like it). Seems pretty damn strange. Blackout, left hand drive, Scotch talk, etc. Had a nice trip. It's cold and raining. Stayed in British barrack.

Date: October 21
Place: Left Ayre, Scotland and went by bus to Glasgow, Scotland. Spent several hours in Glasgow. Traveled by train thru C----, England to Stone, England.

Date: October 21, 1944
Place: 154 Replacement Depot – Stone, England
Lived here in English billets. Had my first experiences in England at pubs, queue's, etc. Did some details. Met my crew again. We're together now.

Date: November 6, 1944
Place: 134 Repl. Bat., 171 Repl. Co. – Paris, France
This is my first real taste of overseas life. Will live in the mud with a tent around us. Food not too hot. Sort of rough.
All the French I know is "Mademoiselle, zig zig, toot sweet." Plenty zig zig, by the way.
We traveled 150 miles in an open truck to the next station. At Bologne we lived at the Chateau Rothchild.

Date: November 11, 1944   A-74
Place: 585 Bomb Sq., 394 Bomb Group, A.P.O. 140, Coueron, France

[November 16, 1944] Promoted to buck sergeant on Novemer 16. Oh boy!!
All set here with my permanent outfit. Not too rough outside of a few missions.
Had a 2-day pass in Paris. Spent 4,000 francs on nothing but it was wonderful. Bumped into Jerry Lowenthal and Bob Christiansen there. Both paddle feet.

[December 1944] Went to Paris the end of December. Good time of course. Beat up on a pro-German girl. She got me very mad speaking against Americans.
Had an air raid but no damage. Paratroopers reported in vicinity

[Date] Dec. 20. Everyone looks like a soldier in field uniform. Guards all over the place.
This German break thru has us all worried. Means rougher missions including fighters.
Plenty more air raid alerts. Germans strafed Cambrai killing several.

[Date] Jan. 18 [1945] received the Air Medal. Feel like a vet now.

[Date] Feb. 21st. [1945] First time this group ever was attacked by fighters. Had lots of flak because of poor navigation thru the fighters. Was a horrible sight. Lost some swell guys. Among them Ampolous. Crews of Hale, Coleman, and Abbott. Hale bailed out, Coleman crash landed and Abbott may have landed.
Plenty new crews here now. Had lots of empty sacks. Sure miss the guys that went down. They may be safe. Hope so.

[Date] February 14, [1945] Lt. Martin and crew had trouble. Three were killed, Red Holland in hospital.

[Date] February 25 [1945] Two ships smash in mid-air while forming. All but one man lost. The remaining members are getting fewer in number. Seems our crew is about the only one left in tact.

[Date] March 1st. [1945] Saw my first crash landing at midnight. Landing gear would not drop. Now wheel twisted. He made a honey of a landing, really a thrill with sparks flashing and him skidding down the runway. No one hurt.

[Date] March 9th. [1945] Promoted to the grade of staff sergeant. Made me feel nice, one year ago I was a private. Always wondered how it would feel to have so many stripes. Now I know but I feel the same.
Been flying like mad since the end of February. I'm sure plenty worn out. A leave would suit me and the crew to a T.

[Date]March 24th. [1945] Expect some kind of D-day on up north at the Rhine. Terrific air action, paratroopers, corp planes, etc.

[Date] March 29th. [1945] The S-2 man told us today we are finished bombing out bridges. There are no more bridges. SOS April 2nd verified this.

[Date] March 30th. [1945] Charlie Rogers and us went to Brussels on a 72-hour. Had the best time so far. Everything was swell. Steak and French fries, ice cream, etc. Wonderful time.

[Date] April 2nd. [1945] We expect the war will be over within a month. Here's hoping.

[Date] April 9th. [1945] Had a damn close call. Ran over a spike while taxing out. On landing we did OK but while taxing in the tire blew. Wow! What luck.

[Date] April 11th. [1945] At briefing they told us to watch out for Russian fighter planes. Went damn far in today.

[Date] April 14th. [1945] Mitchell and I went to Nice on the French Riviera. It was the next thing to home. Were gone 9 days. Had just about everything we wanted. Even American beer.

[Date] April 25. [1945] Packed bag and baggage and left for Y-55. Was hard packing but ? to get out of smelly, ? ?. Came by plane on advance party. Worked pretty hard clearing land and putting up tents, etc. Rained all the damn time.
Every time someone landed here we told them there were snipers in the area etc.

Date: April 27th. [1945] Y-55.
Place: Venlo, Holland on the German border
This is a huge airfield. Had about 125 hangars. We were working hard getting the place ready for the gang. Lots of fine chocolate. The whole field is a large tent city now. Venlo is a helluva town.

[Date June 5, 1945?] Manny left June 5th. He certainly is a swell guy and was a great buddy. Hope to meet him some day. Likewise for Rick.
Not a damn thing to do in Venlo. Been going bugs here with all the sack time. Lately we've had a little ground school, P.T., and stuff. Still pull guard every 5 days.

[Date] June 19th. [1945] We were up flying on instruments and shooting landings, etc. Came down, circled the runway, pre-flighted and started to take off. Going down the runway she wouldn't gain speed. ¾ the way down at about 110 m.p.h. the left engine killed dead. Mr. Kinnon jammed on the brakes. Doyle and I knew something was wrong. We were already braced. Thought we'd roll over and crash sure as hell. Luck was with us. We stopped here at the edge of the grass.

[Date] June 28th. [1945] They called several of us high mission men into operations. Said our orders are going in for return to Z.T(?) Had three choices, 1) active theater, 2) occupation, or 3) no preference (my choice). Supposed to leave in a couple days. I'm skeptical about it all – too good to be true.

[Date] July 2nd. [1945] Was too good to be true. Six men were scratched in preference for men with relatives in Germany. I incidentally was 6th.

[Date] July 3rd. [1945] Dick Hoyle, Charlie Rogers, Chuck Bra? et al - ? I don't feel any too good about it. I have more missions and less point though. Made a mistake by going into operations while all hot. Gave the C.O., a colonel, and the operations officer a bad time. They could have made it rough on me but didn't. I apologized to the colonel on my own volition. He said I should be leaving "soon." I wonder!?!?

My [Alan I. Rubens] Missions
1/ November 18, 1944
2/ November 19, 1944 - Permasens, Germany

3/ November 19, 1944 - Unknown

4/ November 21, 1944 - Unknown

Local flights November 23 & 26

Spare – December 5 – 1 hour 20 minutes

Spare – December 8 – 2 hours 20 minutes

5/ December 10, 1944 – 2 hours Husums, Germany

6/ December 11, 1944 – 2 ½ hours Wieback, Germany

7/ December 12, 1944 – 3 ½ hours Defended city of Wieback. No flak, no bombs.

8/ December 15, 1944 - Spare on a milk run. What luck!

9/ December 23, 1944 – Hit Prum, Germany marshalling yard. Very important target to Germans. Roughest mission so far. Our greatest losses to date but was worth the effort.

10/ December 24, 1944 – Important bridge at Trier. Rough but not as yesterday's.

11/ December 25, 1944 – Bridge far in Germany. Milk run. Successful.

12/ December 25, 1944 – St. With, Belgium marshalling yard. No flak, no bombs.

12B/ December 27, 1944 – Hauffilize communication and supply center. Plenty flak, rough! Rough!

January 4 –No credit, flew near Bastogne. No flak, no bombs.

14/ January 14 – Bridge near St. With. No bombs bust most intense flak to date. Really was worried. See clipping.

15/ January 29 – Defended city of Schonberg, Germany. No bombs, no flak, "bo-coups" cold.

16/ February 3rd – City of Wittlich, Germany. Secondary G-box target. Caught pretty good flak from primary but didn't drop. Too intense. Secondary had no flak. One good hole in right wing. Two 2,000 lb. bombs.

17/ February 6th. Badgladbach, Germany ordnance depot, very important target. Bombed with good cloud coverage, very light flak but expected the works because we passed Trier, Cologne, and Coblence, and Ruhr Valley.

18/ February 9th. Rheydt, Germany. Very important marshalling yard. Hit it, very light flak.

19/ February 10th. Munstinerfel. An ordnance repair shop, quite important. Took pictures, nice weather. Flak moderate, inaccurate.

20/ February 16th. Solingen, Germany. Good weather, not cold – good visibility. Hit a jet prop. factory. P-47s strafed flak guns – hit target.

21/ February 19th. Neuwied, Germany railroad bridge. Flew window a darn good deal. Lost one ship. Moderate flak, two 2,000 lbs. bombs.

22/ February 21st. Hlotho(?), Germany bridge. Weser River 15 miles south of Minden. Never to be forgotten – fighter attack and plenty flak. Lost 3 ships. Made emergency landing at A-91 in Belgium. Could not fly our plane back.

23/ February 24th. Blatzheim, Germany. Defended city with tanks parked in it. Flew window.

24/ Paper mission in Trier vicinity. Two flak bursts.

25/ February 25th. Colbe, Germany. Along the old Cologne, Coblence, Trier route. Milky as all hell. Railroad bridge – 2,000 lbs. 4 hr. 15 min.

26/ February 28th. Camps(?) Germany. Window lead – milk run – Supported Canadian 1st and U.S. 9th Armies.

27/ March 1st. Rheinbach, Germany. Good mission, not too long. Light flak. Returned at 10 p.m.

28/ March 2nd. Giessen, Germany. Hit by a fighter and flak. No damage. Ordnance depot.

29/ March 3rd. Lenz bridge near Sinzig. Window lead – no flak. Took off 9:30, landed 11:30. Toot suite.

30/ March 6th. Dortsmund, Germany. Flew window lead, a marshalling yard near Canadian 1st. Moderate and inaccurate flak.

31 & 32/ March 11th. Hit an air field in the A.M. Dulenberg, Germany and a marshalling hard in the P.M. MILK RUNS! Not a burst of flak, short missions too. # near Dursburg, Germany.

33/ March 12th. Window lead * on a milk run. Hit a * military installation at *. Been 10/10 the lat few days. Near Dolma, Germany.

34/ March 13th. Dustern(?) Germany marshalling yard. Caught flak over Rhine. Short and not much flak elsewhere.

35/ March 14th. Schaafheim, Germany. Air field, perfect visibility, could have been a milk run but poor navigation brought flak.

36/ March 15th. Window lead on a milk run. Hit Nuenkerchen(?), Germany. In the air 2 hours.

37/ March 17th. Altenkerchen(?), Germany. Milk run.

38/ Got screwed up in Germany account of weather so turned back. Credit!!

39/ March 18th. Worms, Germany. Light and accurate. Window lead.

40/

41/ March 22nd. Haltern, Germany. Moderate and accurate. Supposed to be window lead but flew #6. Two ships made emergency landings.

42/ March 23rd. Dinslaken, Germany. Defended city – troops and supplies. Moderate and accurate, 2 hr. 23 min. total time.

43/ March 24th. Bocholt, Germany. No flak but sweated plenty. Expected intense and accurate. Briefing was 5:45 p.m.

44/ April 6th. Arnsberg, Germany. Paper mission. Short and sweet. Hoyal flew with Richards crew and they crash landed!

45/ April 8th. Northeast of Hannover. Good accurate flak for 30 seconds. Scared plenty! Flew tail for first time since #3. Briefing 6 a.m. Engine time 4 p.m. Mission 4 hr. 20 min.

46/ April 9th. Lehrte, Germany 6 min. east. Oil dump near Hannover. Was a milk run but long. Engine time was 5 p.m. and landed about 10 p.m.! Had a blowout after we started taxing in. Lucky!

47/ April 11th. Asiherlaben? Germany. Marshalling yard. Damn far in. Made three runs but finally hit it. No flak. Took 4 ½ hr. on the ??

48/ April 12th. Kempten, Germany. Bad weather so turned back. Got credit.

BOMBS AWAY!
MY LIFE AND TRAINING AS A B-26 PILOT

is archived at the following locations:
The International Archive of the B-26 Marauder Historical Society
University of Akron, Ohio University Library
2255 Main Street, Room LL-10, Akron, Ohio 44325

Andrew Doehly, B-26 Marauder Historian
2900 Timrod Road, Tucson, Arizona 85711.

Chattanooga Hamilton County Bicentennial Library
1001 Broad Street, Chattanooga, Tennessee 37402

To order, please send the information below along with a check or money order for $29.95 plus tax and shipping to: Ed Ryon, P.O. Box 21143, Chattanooga, TN 37424.

Name_____

Shippingaddress_____

_____ Zip _____

Phone_____E-mail(optional)_____

_____ number of books @ $29.95 $_____
Tennessee residents add sales tax @ 9.25% $_____
Ship first book $4.60; each additional @ $3.00 $_____
                    TOTAL enclosed $_____

Mail to: Ed Ryon, P.O. Box 21143, Chattanooga, TN 37424

AUTHOR BIOGRAPHY

Edward L. Ryon
Chattanooga, Tennessee
Primary: Fort Worth, Texas
Basic: Coffeyville, Kansas

First lieutenant Edward Lindsay Ryon, Sr. was born in Chattanooga, Tennessee on March 11, 1923. His family lived at the foot of Lookout Mountain until he was two years of age. At that time, they moved to East Brainerd, a rural area about ten miles east of the city. He started grammar school at the age of 5 ½ at East Brainerd Elementary School. From there, he attended Tyner Junior High and Tyner High School until his graduation in 1941. During high school, he was active in sports, especially varsity football where he served as a co-captain. He was the recipient of the Sons of the American Revolution Award in his senior year.

As a boy growing up during the Depression, Ed would work as a farm hand during the summer. He also worked in a grocery store delivering groceries. On January 31, 1936, Ed became a Boy Scout and was quite active for many years as a Scout Master and leader in the Scouting program.

He attended Concord Baptist Church from the age of two. He became a Christian and joined the church at the age of ten and has been a member at Concord Baptist for

74 years. As a member at Concord, he and his wife, Margaret, took an active part in all phases of the church. He was an ordained deacon, was a Sunday school teacher for twenty years, and worked with the youth. He also served as a trustee and helped write the bylaws and constitution of the church.

He always liked the outdoors and was an avid hunter and fisherman. For many years, he raised and trained bird dogs as well as beagles. He hunted as much as possible. Camping was another favorite outdoor activity. At home, he likes to work outdoors gardening, tending to the many flowers that surround their house. He also enjoys wood working and has a shop at home.

On returning to Chattanooga after the war, Ed and Margaret moved back to the community where they both grew up. Soon after his return, he started working for Southern Bell. He worked there until his retirement in November, 1985. He also attended the University of Chattanooga at night, majoring in civil engineering.

As time permitted, he became active in community affairs. He was involved with the Telephone Pioneers and the Brainerd Optimist Club where he served as a trustee. He taught in the Chattanooga Literacy Movement and taught conversational English to immigrants. He assisted in fund-raising for the Birth Defects Center at T.C. Thompson Children's Hospital where his wife, Margaret, was Executive Director for twenty-five years. He also raised funds for the National Foundation for the March of Dimes.

Now, he enjoys his time in the yard and time with his family which has expanded to include grandchildren and great-grandchildren.

Warnock Pro on Rose 50# white. Type and design by Karen Stone.